Bruce Gunkle's background as an all star athlete, as an air force officer, as a prophet, intercessor, teacher, and pastor has given him a depth of experience and a deep concern regarding the lack of the church's understanding about the power and the anointing of the blood covenant. Bruce Gunkle is a revelatory teacher. This book goes beyond knowledge and insight — it is a prophetic book for this time and age. This book takes you from seeing covenant as a temporal agreement to understanding that covenant is a lifestyle with purpose and conviction.

Because of the lack of true covenant, when one falls, no one is there to pull them up. Relationships are broken and not restored. Only when we stand in true covenant can we walk together for the Kingdom of God and be effective world changers. This book is essential for every Christian who desires a deeper, more committed walk with Christ. Walking in the fullness of covenant reality will yield greater power in your life.

John P. Kelly

CEO, LEAD
Leadership Education for Apostolic Development

Overseeing Apostle, ICA
International Coalition of Apostles

BLOOD COVENANT

BRUCE GUNKLE

BLOOD COVENANT

WALK OF DEATH

What Jesus
Really Did For Us

PALM●TREE
PUBLICATIONS
A Division of Palm Tree Productions

BLOOD COVENANT

PUBLISHED BY PALM TREE PUBLICATIONS
A DIVISION OF PALM TREE PRODUCTIONS
KELLER, TEXAS U.S.A.
PRINTED IN THE U.S.A. | SECOND PRINTING JULY 2012

www.palmtreeproductions.com

Palm Tree Productions is a Media Services Company dedicated to seeing the Kingdom of God advanced by ministries and businesses with excellence, integrity and professionalism through the use of high quality media resources. Whether the publication is print, audio, or visual, we are dedicated to excellence in every aspect from concept to final production.

It is our desire that this publication will enrich your life and cause you to increase in wisdom and understanding.

For more information about products and services available through Palm Tree Productions, visit our website at www.palmtreeproductions.net.

To contact the author, visit
www.thecityofrefuge.org

TABLE OF CONTENTS

FORWARD

Bruce Gunkle is a retired Air Force Lt. Colonel. Upon leaving military service in 1984, he went into the ministry. In 1990 he founded the City of Refuge Christian Fellowship in San Antonio, Texas where he continues to serve as Senior Pastor. In the early 1980's, Bruce was exposed to several insightful teachings on the blood covenant. One in particular strongly impacted him. It was a magazine article written by Pastor Mike Haley from Oklahoma and entitled, "The Great Exchange." Pastor Mike has since gone on to be with the Lord.

Through Mike's article, published in *Fulness Magazine*, the Lord began to unfold the truth about covenant found within the pages of the Bible. As Bruce began to explore the power and promise of the subject, many thought he went a little overboard. One pastor even accused him of reading the Bible through *'covenant colored'* glasses. But eventually, others began to have their eyes opened and see God's amazing provision for them, revealed in the true understanding of covenant.

In the first chapter of this book, Bruce will share with you the insights gleaned from Mike Haley and the remainder of the material comes from revelation given to Bruce by the Holy Spirit over the ensuing years. His purpose for penning this book is to share a vital truth with you that seems to have been stolen from the American church. As a result, the Biblical truths have often been watered down, and many doctrines have been created resulting in weak, uncommitted, and lethargic Christians who perish for lack of knowledge.

As you read this book, pray that the eyes of your understanding will be opened and that you will enter into the promises and power of God's Covenant.

INTRODUCTION

Jehovah is a covenant God and historically relates to men through the covenants He makes with them. Most people have an awareness of both the Old and New Covenants, and some have studied the covenants He made specifically with Adam, Noah, David and others.

Present day American Christianity has one patent weakness. This weakness is readily apparent when you look closely at scripture. The church in America does not understand covenant and, therefore, does not understand much of what the Lord is saying in scripture. It is not possible to fully grasp what the Bible is all about without reading it through *'covenant colored'* glasses.

For example, we casually talk and even sing songs about being the friend of God. Yet the term *friend* in the Bible is not just a reference to a special acquaintance, but rather, the term *friend* refers to a faithful covenant partner who is dedicated to **my good**, and vice versa. This type of relationship transcends what we know and understand as friendship today. It rises to the level of commitment where we are required (and are willing) to lay down our life for each other. There is nothing casual about it. It is a **purposeful** and **determined** relationship.

In the world of the blood covenant, there is no such thing as independence from one another, or being a loner. Covenant is a realm of commitment, involvement, and preferring one another. It is a place where we are literally dead to ourselves, our desires, and our way so that we can live for the kingdom of God — which includes all our covenant co-workers.

This book is not designed to be a totally exhaustive study of covenant. It is an attempt to whet your appetite so you will delve more deeply into this truth of paramount importance that has been stolen from the church. Hopefully, as you read this book, you will see the scripture through *new* eyes. Then the revelation of this truth will consume you as you adjust your Christian journey, armed with a new depth of understanding of **what it's all about**.

Chapter One

UNDERJTANDING BLOOD COVENANT

If you ask today's regular church going people about blood covenant, most are clueless about what it means. You will also find that those who *think* they know, are not very well versed on the subject. They may have studied biblical covenants, and to some extent have knowledge about covenants *(Noahic, Davidic, Abrahamic, etc.)*, but they don't really understand covenant.

The Bible is a book of covenants, the Old and New Testaments are really the Old and New Covenants. In addition, there are numerous references where there were covenants between men, and covenants between God and men. Much of the Bible is written in covenant terminology and involves covenant principles. So, in order to understand the Bible, one *must* have an understanding of covenant. This will help us be more clear about what the Bible is talking about.

Because of their ignorance regarding covenant, Christians in general are somewhat hamstrung in exercising their Christian faith. Even some of the most well known biblical passages are misconstrued because of covenantal implications that are missed by the reader or that simply go over their heads. Because of traditionally established thought patterns, it is difficult to stretch beyond the logical and superficial interpretations that religious culture has programmed them with.

Again, the devil has struck a spiritual blow against Christians that seriously affects them. Because covenant is so important, the devil has worked overtime to steal an understanding of it, and to cause those who do enter into covenant not to be faithful to the terms of the covenant. This can be seen symbolically as early in the Old Testament as Genesis 15 where the birds (representing our old enemy, the devil) come down and try to steal pieces of the sacrificial animal to deter the process of making covenant.

Basic to covenant is marriage — because marriage is a blood covenant. Many of the problems in marriages today, and the numerous divorces that result, could possibly have been averted had the average Christian been armed with a practical, working understanding of true covenant.

What was done for us at Calvary has *everything* to do with covenant. Jesus, as our substitute, cut a blood covenant with the Father on our behalf. As a result, we have established a covenant relationship with Him — not to mention accruing a multitude of blessings and benefits!

God has dealt with man through covenants from the very beginning. Adam and Eve were covered by the skin of a sacrificed animal, indicating that they were indoctrinated into the understanding of blood covenant. The Hebrew word for covenant, *beriyth*, means to cut, with the implication of the flowing of blood. In nearly every place in scripture where the word *beriyth* is used it literally means to "*cut a covenant.*" Hence, the term blood covenant (*there are other type covenants such as a salt covenant*). Many primitive peoples in different parts of the world today practice blood covenant — and although it is not exactly the same, the ritual followed in nearly all cases have striking similarities.

UNDERSTANDING BLOOD COVENANT

Although there are other types of binding covenants (as previously mentioned) we will speak in general about blood covenants. In a blood covenant there is the cutting or dividing of a sacrifice (animal), which is indicative of the serious intent and ultimate commitment involved for the one entering a blood covenant. There is a binding oath whereby a person dies to himself, putting the covenant partner even above himself — i.e. preferring the other (Philippians 2:3-4). This is reflected in our daily lives even in regard to our natural possessions. When you are in a covenant relationship, everything we have is theirs and vice-versa. In fact, Proverbs indicates that the blood brother becomes closer and more important than even a natural family member (Proverbs 18:24).

Technically, when we accept Jesus we go into covenant with Him and partake of the covenant He made on our behalf with the Father. At the same time, we are in covenant **with all others who are also in covenant with Jesus — and with the Father** (John 17:20-23). So, we are under covenant obligation to lay everything down not only for the Lord, but also for our earthly covenant brothers. This may involve merely our time or possessions, but could also involve our very lives (1 John 3:16-17).

To best describe covenant so that you will appreciate the seriousness of it and have a working understanding of it, we will explore the steps ancient Hebrews actually went through in the process of *cutting covenant*. These steps are very revealing symbolically, and will be carefully elaborated in the next few pages. You will see that the process is very messy and particularly bloody, which is purposeful. It is a stark reminder to the participants of the *death* that they are to experience, literally giving their life away to their new covenant partner. In addition, this all takes place in front of witnesses.

Step One
The Exchange of Robes

The first step in cutting covenant involved an exchange of coats. The coat represented one's identity — in other words, it was all that they were. This exchange symbolized the putting on of one another, as each person took on the identity of the other. It was also an exchange of ownership which included an exchange of names or even a name change. Notice that *Abram* became *Abraham* and that the *Lord* became the *God of Abraham*. Abram changed His name to include the **ah** from Y**ah**weh — much like the wife takes on the name of the husband.

Those making covenant stand in front of witnesses, reading a list of their possessions. This, in essence, declares, "All that I have, all that is mine is now yours." Everything that belonged to one now belonged to the other also. For instance, in marriage, it is not meant to be *my money* and *your money*, it is all *our money*. Also in marriage, there is no longer *my body*. Once I have entered into the marriage covenant, my body now belongs to the covenant partner (1 Corinthians 7:3-5).

> *All that I have, all that is mine — is now yours.*

It should be noted that the decision to go into covenant with someone should be very carefully considered. You are literally giving yourself away. You need to be careful with whom you are going to make such a serious commitment. That is the true purpose of the engagement period preceding marriage. It is a time to really get to know the one you will potentially partner with for the rest of your life. There's no going back, as this decision involves total commitment.

We can see this in the covenant we have with (*in*) Him. The Lord takes who we are (*our filthy rags/fallen state*) and gives us the white robes of righteousness (Isaiah 61:10). Jesus actually took on the identity of a human, able to feel as we do, able even to be tempted as we are. This made it possible for Him to die for us so we could partake of His divine nature. This is stated even better in 2 Corinthians.

He made Him who knew no sin
to be sin on our behalf, so that we might
become the righteousness of God in Him.
— 2 Corinthians 5:21 NASU —

Step Two
The Exchange of the Belt and Weapons

This step is clearly enumerated in 1 Samuel 18:1-3 where we see Jonathan and David making covenant. The exchange of the belt, which girds, is a symbol of strength. The weapons, which are attached to the belt, symbolize the ability to fight. So together, this exchange means that should there be a need, all one's strength and one's ability to fight are at the disposal of the other.

All my strength and ability to fight are yours.

Otherwise stated, it means that wherever I am strong and you are weak, I have your back — I've got you covered. All your friends are now my friends and all your enemies are now my enemies and vice versa. We are totally in this together for better or for worse. We will lay down our lives, if necessary, to fulfill the covenant vow. This is seen in Joshua 9 and 10 where the Israelites were required by God to go help defend the Gibeonites who were being attacked by the five kings of the Amorites. Since Joshua and the leaders of Israel had recently made covenant with the Gibeonites, there was a covenant obligation to come to their aid.

In our covenant with the Lord, the battle is His (1 Samuel 17:47). Wherever we are weak, the Lord assures us that He will be strong for us.

And He has said to me, "My grace is sufficient for you, for power is perfected in weakness." Most gladly, therefore, I will rather boast about my weaknesses, so that the power of Christ may dwell in me.

Therefore I am well content with weaknesses, with insults, with distresses, with persecutions, with difficulties, for Christ's sake; for when I am weak, then I am strong.

— 2 Corinthians 12:9-10 NASU —

Step Three
The Cutting of the Sacrificial Animal

When making a blood covenant, a sacrificial animal was literally cut in half and the two parts were laid down apart from each other. This is demonstrated in Genesis 15 when God made a covenant with Abraham, promising him an heir and a nation. The ritual was carried out as Abraham brought God a heifer, a goat and a ram, cut them in half and laid the pieces opposite from one another. The Bible shows then that a smoking pot and a flaming torch passed between the animals representing God, the Father, and God, the Son (*Jesus*).

When the Hebrews cut covenant, a sacrificial animal would be cut down the middle and the two pieces would be laid side by side. The individuals making covenant would stand in

If I break this covenant, may this be done to me.

the midst of this bloody mess (between the two pieces), and swear before God to keep their part of the covenant. If they broke the covenant, then what was done to the animal would be done to them. This symbolized the total commitment demanded of someone in covenant. It indicated a total death to themselves and a being alive to the other one. In fact, in Hebrews 9:16-17 it states that a covenant is valid only when men are dead.

> *For where a covenant is, there*
> *must of necessity be the death*
> *of the one who made it.*
>
> *For a covenant is valid only when*
> *men are dead, for it is never in force*
> *while the one who made it lives.*
>
> *— Hebrews 9:16 - 17 NASU—*

We were slaves to sin but now we are slaves to righteousness. We are His bondslaves, and must seek the kingdom first (Matthew 6:33), dying to the world, our old ways and our desires. We are not our own. We have been bought with a price.

> *Or do you not know that your body*
> *is a temple of the Holy Spirit who is*
> *in you, whom you have from God,*

and that you are not your own?
For you have been bought with a price:
therefore glorify God in your body.

— 1 Cor 6:19-20 NASU —

Step Four

The Walk of Death

The soon-to-be covenant partners then walk in what is termed the walk of blood or the walk of death. They walk a figure eight around and through both pieces. Interestingly, the number eight signifies new beginnings — and that is what takes place. There is a new future where each will prefer the other by putting them first (Philippians 2:3-4). A mutual death is taking place, giving rise to new life in the form of the new covenant relationship.

This is a picture of a dying daily that allows two people to walk side by side in complete oneness. It says, for instance, in Luke 9 that we are to take up our cross daily and follow Him.

And He was saying to them all,
"If anyone wishes to come after Me,
he must deny himself, and take up
his cross daily and follow Me."

— Luke 9:23-24 NASU —

We die to our old self. We die to our wants and desires. We walk a walk of repentance that will take us out of ourselves and more into Him.

The secret to being a faithful covenant partner to the

Lord and to our Christian brothers is to remove ourselves from the equation. We must learn that it is not about us, but rather that it is about Him and His kingdom.

The term *friend* in the Bible does not have the same meaning today as it did back in biblical days. Today it is used indiscriminately and the word *friend* can refer to a life-long comrade, or just as easily to a casual acquaintance. In Bible days, *friend* referred to covenant partners. This fact will help explain what John 15:14 means. We are true friends (covenant partners) with the Lord when we die to our ways and live His way.

> *"You are My friends if you do*
> *what I command you.*
>
> — *John 15:14* NASU —

Step Five
The Striking of the Hands

This step required the participants to cut their right wrists just short of the palm, so that blood would flow. Then they would shake hands, grasping each other's arms. This positions the bleeding wrists next to each other and allows the blood from the wounds to flow back and forth. This symbolizes that these two have become one; they have exchanged lives; they are no longer two, but one.

We are no longer two. Now we are one.

Notice that the blood intermingles. There is no separation; there is complete oneness. There is no undoing or going back. The covenant deal is sealed until physical death. In fact, the covenant partners are closer than their own natural families.

A man of too many friends comes to ruin, But there is a friend who sticks closer than a brother.

— Proverbs 18:24 NASU —

In ancient times, the wrist wound was roughed up and made to scar badly. Then, when someone was threatened or in trouble they would proudly display the scars in the raising of the hands. This warned the one making a threat that he had better be careful – for there was evidently a covenant partner he would have to deal with should harm come to the one with the scars. Hence, today we have the raising of hands when one surrenders.

This step is also where the tradition of shaking hands came from. What this originally meant in the covenant ritual was that, *"I'll bless you if it kills me."*

Step Six
The Pronouncing of Blessings and the Curses

In front of witnesses, each of the participants would pronounce blessings for being a faithful covenant partner and curses should for any reason he not keep covenant. This would include speaking the blessings and curses over their respective families.

Deuteronomy 28, for example, lists the blessings and curses of the Old Covenant. Covenant involves total commitment and there were blessings for keeping covenant and curses for breaking it. This is particularly true of our covenant with God. Disobedience (*or sin*) takes us out of good covenant standing and certain penalties (*or curses*) will accompany our disobedience. This is a judgment for not being faithful to the covenant. On the other hand, obedience brings blessings as indicated in Deuteronomy 28:2.

Our New Covenant blessings include all Jesus has, since we are joint heirs with Him.

...and if children, heirs also, heirs of God and fellow heirs with Christ, if indeed we suffer with Him so that we may also be glorified with Him.

— Romans 8:17 NASU —

Step Seven
The Covenant (Memorial) Meal

In this final step, the two men took bread and wine together. In turn, one would take a piece of bread, dip it into the wine, and feed it to the other one. Obviously, this was significant of the oneness that they were entering. This is where one of the traditions we often see at a wedding originated. During the reception, it is normal for the bride to feed the groom a piece of the wedding cake, and he then does the same to her.

We often partake of the covenant meal with our Christian brothers and sisters when we take communion (*the Lord's Supper*). In this act we are renewing our commitment to Him and the covenant He made for us. We reaffirm our commitment to Him as well as to all others who also are in covenant with Him. After all, all His friends are our friends (*step two of covenant listed before*).

Is not the cup of blessing which we bless a sharing in the blood of Christ? Is not the bread which we break a sharing in the body of Christ?

— 1 Corinthians 10:16 NASU —

*You cannot drink the cup of the
Lord and the cup of demons; you
cannot partake of the table of the
Lord and the table of demons.*

— *1 Corinthians 10:21 NASU* —

As previously stated, the covenant ritual varied depending on the tradition or culture. Some used other memorials, rather than, or in addition to, the covenant meal. Trees planted, a memorial pile of rocks, or a memorial herd were common. All were designed to be a reminder of the covenant, much like the wedding ring is used today.

Summary

As you can see there is much more to being a Christian than saying a prayer, going to church, and getting blessed. It is serious business — *covenant business,* and we determine whether we will have the hand of God *for us* in blessing, or *against us* for stepping outside of covenant. We are not to be the same as we were before entering into the covenant with God. Our old self (*the I, me part*) dies and the new, covenant-keeping self arises to walk with the Lord and with our other covenant, Christian brothers. This understanding of covenant also helps us to understand the importance of our marriage vows, realizing that God does in fact *hate* divorce. Divorce is the result of broken covenant. When we walk in true understanding of covenant, our eyes are not on ourselves, but on the kingdom, and on our brothers in Christ. We have an obligation to meet their needs in the time of distress (1 John 3:16-17), and we will not speak against them or come against them, realizing that when we do, we touch Him (Matthew 25:40).

Chapter Two

IN THE NAME

We have learned that the first step of the ancient ritual of covenant was an **exchange of robes**. This signified an exchange of all that we were and all that we owned. Those making the covenant literally gave themselves away "lock, stock and barrel" to their new covenant partner — and their new partner did the same to them. When the exchange of robes was complete, they owned everything that belonged to their partner, and their partner owned everything that was theirs.

This was confirmed by an **exchange of names**. This name change is a picture of what was happening as a result of entering into covenant. There was a combining, or a going into each other. For example, if elder Rob Wallace and I, Bruce Gunkle, were to perform the ritual, we would exchange names in this fashion; he would become Robert *Gunkle* Wallace and I would become Bruce *Wallace* Gunkle. In ancient times, an exchange of names was made so that the names of those entering into covenant became intermeshed, much the same as their identities. This signified that those in covenant were now one — inseparable.

Notice that this was what happened between Abram and the Lord (**Yah**weh). Abram's name became Abr**ah**am and the Lord became the *God of* Abraham. Abram included in his name the <u>*ah*</u>, from Y**ah**weh, much like when a wife takes on the name of her husband. This symbolized the new identity. Neither party remained solo, but now included the identity of the other one also. The two were actually tied or united as one.

When we are born again, the Bible **requires us** to be water baptized.

Go therefore and make disciples of all the nations, **baptizing them in the name of** *the Father and the Son and the Holy Spirit,*

— Matthew 28:19 NASU —

This involves us being baptized in (**into**) the name of the Father (*Lord*), Son (*Jesus*) and Holy Ghost (*Christos*) — *the anointing*) in Matthew 28:19. So we are actually baptized (*into*) in the name of the Lord Jesus Christ when we are buried with Him in baptism.

Or do you not know that all of us who have been baptized into Christ Jesus have been baptized into His death? Therefore we have been buried with Him through baptism into death, so that as Christ was raised from the dead through the glory of the Father, so we too might walk in newness of life. For if we have become united with Him in the likeness of His death, certainly we shall also be in the likeness of His resurrection, knowing this, that our old self was crucified with Him, in order that our body of sin might

be done away with, so that we would no
longer be slaves to sin; for he who has
died is freed from sin.

— *Romans 6:3-7 NASU* —

Here we see that we are baptized **into** Him — buried with Him, united with Him in the likeness of His death, and also in the likeness of His resurrection. We become one with Him and upon coming out of the water have a **newness** of life with Him. We are raised with Him from death with a circumcised heart that is capable of putting off the flesh and walking as one with Him — in His Name.

...and in Him you were also circumcised
with a circumcision made without hands,
in the removal of the body of the flesh by
the circumcision of Christ; having been
buried with Him in baptism, in which you
were also raised up with Him through
faith in the working of God, who raised
Him from the dead.

— *Colossians 2: 11-12 NASU* —

We have talked about the exchange of robes and about the exchange of names giving us a new identity. That's what we are talking about here in baptism. In baptism, we are clothed with Him, giving up our old identity (*our old man*) and our sinful nature to embrace Him. We are united with Him and are **clothed** with the **white robes of righteousness** (Isaiah 61:10). All this was made possible for us because Jesus willingly was our substitute, taking on our sin, our debt — a covenant exchange which only love can explain.

*For all of you who were baptized
into Christ have **clothed** yourselves
with Christ.*

— *Galatians 3:27* NASU —

In Ephesians 5 the scripture says that marriage (*a blood covenant*) is to be like Christ and the church. It is not surprising then that in the marriage ceremony, the wife goes into the name of the husband. She is no longer identified with her birth family, but becomes one with her husband in a *new* family (*her covenant family*). So, the wife takes on the husband's name. When my wife and I got married, she was no longer identified as Sherry Godwin. Her name went into my name and she became identified as Sherry Godwin Gunkle.

*The devil
HATES
covenant!*

The devil *hates* covenant — he passionately abhors covenant! He tries to interfere with *any* attempt at making a godly blood covenant. He hates the covenant oneness that marriage can potentially produce. That's why we see a trend among some modern, independent women not to take the name of their husband. They often try to retain their *own* identity by keeping their *own* name. On the surface it seems harmless, but in reality, it is a reflection of making a lesser commitment than true covenant requires.

*For where a covenant is, there must of
necessity be the death of the one who
made it. For a covenant is valid **only**
when men are dead, for it is **never** in
force while the one who made it lives.*

— *Hebrews 9:16-17* NASU —

In our covenant with Jesus, we are to go ***into the Name*** at water baptism and are to <u>remain</u> ***in the Name***. This means that we submit to Him through our obedience, and as we obey, we abide in Him (*in His Name*). In essence, we are dying to our desires and our way in order to live for Him and His ways.

When we do this we are in good covenant standing, and can expect all the blessings of covenant to come our way (Deuteronomy 28:2), and can anticipate that Jesus will be quick to respond to our prayers and needs.

*...and whatever we ask we receive from Him, because we **keep** His commandments and **do** the things that are pleasing in His sight.*

This is His commandment, that we believe in the name of His Son Jesus Christ, and love one another, just as He commanded us.

The one who keeps His commandments abides in Him, and He in him. We know by this that He abides in us, by the Spirit whom He has given us.

— 1 John 3:22-24 NASU —

All these blessings will come upon you and overtake you if you obey the LORD your God:

— Deuteronomy 28: 2 NASU —

It has become a widely practiced custom to put the phrase, "in the Name of Jesus" at the end of every prayer.

It is used like a rubber stamp that is supposed to make the prayer more spiritual and acceptable. Why do so many Christians do this? Actually, this practice arose out of a misinterpretation of what the scripture says. Let's look at John 16:23-24 as an example.

> *In that day you will not question Me about anything. Truly, truly, I say to you, if you ask the Father for anything in **My name**, He will give it to you.*
>
> *Until now you have asked for nothing in My name; ask and you will receive, so that your joy may be made full.*
>
> *— John 16:23-24 NASU —*

Basically, the verses here say that we are now in covenant and, as a result, have access to the Father. When Jesus died on the cross, He rent the veil in the Temple that separated God from man. We can now approach the Throne just like the Israelites could approach the Ark of the Covenant in the Tabernacle of David (1 Chronicles 16:1).

We go **into the Name** at water baptism, but we must be standing in His name in order to meet the requirements of this verse. Stated otherwise, we are to be **abiding** (*living*) in Him as seen in 1 John 3:24 above. This equates to our being dead to ourselves and alive to Him (*obedient and submissive*). Then we are in good covenant standing (*in His Name*) to have all our needs and possibly even our wants met.

This is quite a change from what most people think this scripture says. Maybe this explains why many of the prayers that are prayed aren't answered. Technically, any prayer prayed in rebellion, prayed in sin, or otherwise prayed while in disobedience, is **not in the Name**. A prayer that is prayed **not** in the Name means that the condition of the verse is not met. If the prayer is prayed **not** in the Name, then He is not obligated to answer. This same condition also explains why the effective prayer of a righteous man accomplishes much (James 5:16). The righteous man, by nature of his walking righteously, **is in His Name**, and therefore in a covenant position to be heard and be blessed.

When you consider this, it helps explain what the Lord was saying to His disciples when He spoke about honoring the request of two or three **gathered in His Name**. For when there was a mutual abiding and agreement about something, there was also His presence and an open line of communication to a covenant God who wants to aid and bless His covenant people.

> *Again I say to you, that if two of you*
> *agree on earth about anything that they*
> *may ask, it shall be done for them by My*
> *Father who is in heaven. For where two*
> *or three have gathered together in My*
> *name, I am there in their midst.*
>
> *— Matthew 18:19-20* NASU *—*

This is particularly important in regard to prayer meetings, especially intercessor's meetings. It mandates that participants *'shake the dust off'* before they gather in a group who intend to agree in prayer. Removing the daily distractions, cares, and offenses solidifies each one's standing in His Name. This guarantees the type of agreement that will produce the powerful impact in the spirit that prayer is for. The idea of the effective prayer of two, three or a group of righteous intercessors standing in His Name terrifies the demonic hordes. That's what unforgiveness, bitterness, jealousy, rejection and all the other junk the devil throws at us is trying to prevent. That's why division is one of his tactics — he wants to **divide** and **conquer**.

The warfare against our covenant with God and our brothers and sisters is relentless, so we must be on alert. At the same time, by virtue of being in covenant with our big Brother Jesus, we have a Friend Who will fight our battles for us. This is what the **exchange of the weapons** was about in the second step of the blood covenant ritual (1 Samuel 18:1-4). That's one of the advantages of being in covenant — **we're not in it by ourselves**, we're not alone. If we have a covenant partner, that partner is committed to be in any of our difficult situations should we need their help.

We are not ALONE!

Look at 1 Samuel 17. David became the one to fight Goliath on behalf of the armies of Israel. He went out to face Goliath, seemingly out gunned and out classed, but he was not alone. The battle wasn't his alone, for he was standing there **in the Name of the Lord.**

*Then David said to the Philistine, "You come to me with a sword, a spear, and a javelin, but I come to you **in the name of the LORD of hosts**, the God of the armies of Israel, whom you have taunted. This day the LORD will deliver you up into my hands, and I will strike you down and remove your head from you. And I will give the dead bodies of the army of the Philistines this day to the birds of the sky and the wild beasts of the earth, that*

all the earth may know that there is a
God in Israel, and that all this assembly
may know that the LORD does not
deliver by sword or by spear;
for the battle is the LORD'S and
He will give you into our hands."

— *1 Samuel 17:45-47* NASU —

It is obvious here that David, who in the natural should have been fearful of Goliath like the rest of Israel, was instead bold and aggressive in his seeking out the giant. Why? Because he knew he had a more powerful covenant Partner Who was much *bigger* and *badder* than Goliath. He knew he had all the resources of heaven on his side — it was all available to him **in His Name**. Once David stated that the battle was the Lord's, the rest was history.

Consider Isaiah 4:1.

For seven women will take hold of one
man in that day, saying, "We will eat our
own bread and wear our own clothes,
only let us be called by your name;
take away our reproach!"

This is an interesting Old Testament scripture that I believe speaks to the ideology of many attending church in this country. They are either ignorant of covenant or they are unconcerned about the commitment that covenant demands.

In this Isaiah scripture, there are a number of covenant implications and an obvious ignorance of the necessity of any covenant commitment. Notice first of all, the desire to receive the benefits of covenant — the desire to be "called by your Name," and especially the desire that all reproach or sin be taken away from them. In other words, the seven women wanted covenant benefits, but on their terms alone. This accurately demonstrates the attitude of much of the American church. That is, "*I* want to do it *my* way and be alive to what *I* want. *I* want to live my life the way *I* choose and *I* want to be blessed besides." It's much easier to just pray the prayer of Jabez and count on whatever blessings you may have need of or think should be coming your way. It is an attempt to have the benefits of covenant without bearing the burden of the responsibilities of covenant relationship.

These seven women were very clear to state what they anticipated doing — wear our **own** clothes and eat whatever **we** want. This reflects a reluctance to die to themselves, not wanting to exchange robes or names. They wanted to maintain their own identity and make no changes to their way of doing things. In addition, their self-will is further exemplified by what they determined to eat. In John 6, Jesus told his followers at that time that they had to eat of Him. Nearly all of them departed upon hearing these words. In this passage (Isaiah 4:1) we have here the same reaction. They have no intention of eating of Him, and they make it clear that they want to partake of the world or whatever else they want.

This demonstrates a lukewarm approach to covenant; one in which there is no dying or sacrifice. It is rather a covenant of convenience that imposes on a loving, yet just God, expecting Him to ignore sin and bless them nonetheless. Many Christians today adopt this same philosophy in practice, even if they don't know how to state it in words. But this violates scripture and a basic truth — a covenant is valid *only* when men are dead (Hebrews 9:17). When Christians refuse to die to themselves, and die to sin, it is impossible to partake of God's covenant.

For God to make covenant with them under these terms would violate His very character. God is a just God, and therefore has to deal with sin. He doesn't have one set of rules for one group of people and a different set of rules for another group of people. He is the Lord, Who changes not. He is the same yesterday, today and forever. Those who will not partake of the WHOLE covenant, cannot choose to partake of selected PIECES of the covenant that they find desirable.

There is a New Testament verse found in Colossians 3 that concisely summarizes our discussion.

Whatever you do in word
or deed, do all in the
name of the Lord Jesus,
giving thanks through Him
to God the Father.

— Colossians 3:17 NASU —

This is what it's all about. This is where we need to be able to position ourselves. This should be our goal as a covenant person. We have to prove ourselves to be a faithful friend through our obedience to all God wants — the way He wants it. Only then will we have truly died to ourselves, and all that we do or say will be dramatically different. We will be standing *in His Name* and our every action would reflect that. We will have the hand of God for us and not against us. We will have the favor of God in all circumstances. We will have both the protection and the blessings of God. We will see the fruit of our labor in the harvest of souls and the accomplishment of all the kingdom work ordained for us. This will be done in His strength and not just ours alone.

*In that day you will not
question Me about anything.
Truly, truly, I say to you, if you
ask the Father for anything
in My name,
He will give it to you.*

— *John 16:23* NASU —

Chapter Three

A ONENE⨍⨍ THAT I⨍ TRUE UNITY

In continuing our discussion about covenant, especially blood covenant, we will look at the issue of unity or oneness. Obviously, this is an integral part of covenant, and it demands **continual commitment** on the part of all those in covenant.

Commitment seems to present a real problem in our culture. The culture of **American Independence** encourages us to be strong in **ourselves**. We desire to emulate people who have pulled themselves up '*by their own bootstraps*,' have overcome obstacles by their determination, and embodied an independent spirit. Commitment to others requires a level of dependence on each other that we somehow find undesireable.

I once communicated some requirements to a church leader that I thought were reasonable, and even pretty standard. His reaction to these requirements surprised me. He told me that he simply couldn't be as committed as I was. I quickly replied that we had to get something straight — there are not *levels* of commitment. In fact, the term **total commitment** is redundant. The word **commitment** by itself means **all the way in** — not part way. You are either committed or you are not committed.

There is no partial commitment. You cannot be less committed or more committed than someone else. This is true of any blood covenant. Remember Hebrews 9:16-17, "There must of necessity be **the death of the one who made the covenant.**" That says it all! Jesus said, "He who is not against you is for you," (Luke 9:50) — there is no middle ground.

Those who are trying to walk the middle ground are deceived. We are either in covenant or not. We are either married or not. We are either members of a church or not. We are either born again or we are not. It is those who are trying to walk in the middle — trying to live with the freedom to do whatever they want — who fit the pattern of the seven women we discussed from Isaiah 4:1. They want covenant relationship on their terms entirely. There is no willingness to die to self, but rather a rebellious, independent decision to remain alive to whatever they choose. These independent souls are the lukewarm ones that the Lord indicates he will vomit out of His mouth in the Laodicean church.

> *I know your deeds, that you are*
> *neither cold nor hot; I wish that you*
> *were cold or hot. So because you are*
> *lukewarm, and neither hot nor cold,*
> *I will spit you out of My mouth.*
>
> *— Revelations 3:15-16 NASU —*

In John 17, Jesus prays to the Father and stresses unity:

> *I do not ask on behalf of these alone, but*
> *for those also who believe in Me through*
> *their word; **that they may all be one;***
> *even as You, Father, are in Me and I in*

You, that they also may be in Us, so that the world may believe that You sent Me.

*The glory which You have given Me I have given to them, **that they may be one, just as We are one;** I in them and You in Me, **that they may be perfected in unity,** so that the world may know that You sent Me, and loved them, even as You have loved Me.*

John 17:20-23 NASU

Here we see Jesus including all who believe because *we are all one* — regardless of color, gender, religious denomination, etc. Once we become a true believer, we are in it together; we have fellowship with Him and with one another (1 John 1:7). We all are His co-workers (1 Corinthians 3:9); fellow heirs with Christ (Romans 8:17; Ephesians 3:6; Hebrews 11:9); seated together in heavenly places with Christ (Ephesians 2:6); and blessed with every spiritual blessing in Christ (Ephesians 1:3).

Psalms 133 is one of the main unity passages in the Bible. We automatically quote or reference this passage when unity is discussed:

Behold, how good and how pleasant it is

For brothers to dwell together in unity!

It is like the precious oil upon the head,

Coming down upon the beard,

Even Aaron's beard,

Coming down upon the edge of his robes.

BLOOD COVENANT

It is like the dew of Hermon

*Coming down upon the
mountains of Zion;*

*For there the LORD commanded
the blessing — life forever*

— Psalm 133 NASU —

The Hebrew word for **pleasant** includes an inference of singing or of something musical. I interpret this as indicating that this type of corporate unity brings with it added blessings of harmony and joy. The word **dwell** means to settle, to marry, or to remain. This implies that it is not a temporary thing, but rather something more long term — a commitment. When this type of unity is seen and experienced, there is an inherent corporate blessing of **life** that is realized because Jesus, Who is one with us, is also in our midst.

True unity experiences the corporate blessing of Jesus dwelling in our midst.

The precious oil on the head that flows down the body (verse 2) is also talking about how the whole body benefits by the covenant unity that comes. The unity experienced encourages and enlarges all from the highest to the lowest (from head to toe) — consecrating the whole body. The result is experiencing the very life and anointing of Jesus, as He is one with us in our midst.

*For where two or three have
gathered together in My name,
I am there in their midst.*

— Matthew 18:20 NASU —

38

It states in 1 Corinthians 12:27, that corporately we are one (because we are Christ's body), yet each of us has a crucial individual part.

But now there are many members, but one body.

And the eye cannot say to the hand, "I have no need of you;" or again the head to the feet, "I have no need of you."

On the contrary, it is much truer that the members of the body which seem to be weaker are necessary; and those members of the body which we deem less honorable, on these we bestow more abundant honor, and our less presentable members become much more presentable, whereas our more presentable members have no need of it.

But God has so composed the body, giving more abundant honor to that member which lacked, so that there may be no division in the body, but that the members may have the same care for one another. And if one member suffers, all the members suffer with it; if one member is honored, all the members rejoice with it.

Now you are Christ's body, and individually members of it...

— 1 Corinthians 12:20-27 NASU—

You see, we are made by the Lord to be a part of one another, having a need for what each other has. According to 1 Corinthians 12:7, our gifts are for the **common good**. So everything we do impacts one another, and we cannot afford any division or breakdown. We need to be an efficiently operating machine that is well oiled (*anointed — Psalms 133*), and functioning in harmony on all cylinders.

It says in Ephesians 4:16 that **every joint supplies** (*you are a joint in the body*) and, so **by this, we grow up together in love**. Do you see the covenant implication? Do you see the terrible results that come from division or separation? Picture your own physical body. What if some of your joints chose not to input or supply their function as God designed them to do? Would your entire body suffer? Of course it would. This is the same in the Body of Christ. When one or more joints chooses not to function as they were designed, the whole body suffers. So, refusing to input for whatever reason — fear, anger, insecurity, unforgiveness — takes away from everyone and lessens the effectiveness of the corporate body.

Proverbs 18:1 (NASU) says that separation is not a good thing:

He who separates himself
seeks his own desire,
He quarrels against all sound wisdom.

This passage is very specific about the result of someone pulling away in self preservation, no longer wanting to function with the rest of the body. That person (*regardless of their motivation for the separation*) is out for himself, alive in that he is placing his needs above those of the body. Through his self-preservation, he is **alive to himself** and won't **lay down his life** for the body. This same verse says that he is not wise in these actions.

This attitude fights the wisdom of God who created us to function together. He designed each of us to have a part that the rest of the body needs (*1 Corinthians 13:9*). Refusing to be an active body part is basically placing your way and your thoughts above God's way and God's thoughts. It is pride. It indicates that you have not died to sin and the flesh, but rather are alive to your own desires and walking outside of God's covenant. So, separation (*self preservation*) inhibits the body from totally functioning as a covenant entity, as well as deprives the body of the resources possessed by every missing joint (wisdom, gifts, etc.).

Since what affects one member affects us all who are in true unity, then sin in the body is a bad thing that must be dealt with. 1 Corinthians 5 says that a little **leaven** (*sin*) **leavens the whole lump** (*the body*).

> *Your boasting is not good.*
> *Do you not know that a little leaven*
> *leavens the whole lump of dough?*
> *Clean out the old leaven so that*
> *you may be a new lump, just as*
> *you are in fact unleavened.*

> *For Christ our Passover also has been*
> *sacrificed. Therefore, let us celebrate the*
> *feast, not with old leaven, nor with the*
> *leaven of malice and wickedness,*
> *but with the unleavened bread*
> *of sincerity and truth.*

> *I wrote you in my letter not to associate*
> *with immoral people; I did not at all mean*
> *with the immoral people of this world, or*

*with the covetous and swindlers, or with
idolaters, for then you would have to go
out of the world. But actually, I wrote to
you not to associate with any so-called
brother if he is an immoral person,
or covetous, or an idolater, or a reviler,
or a drunkard, or a swindler —
not even to eat with such a one.*

**For what have I to do with judging
outsiders? Do you not judge those
who are within the church? But those
who are outside, God judges.
REMOVE THE WICKED MAN FROM
AMONG YOURSELVES.**

— 1 Corinthians 5:6-13 NASU —

We are to be a holy people as He is holy (*1 Peter 1:15*),
and His will is for our sanctification (*1 Thessalonians 4:3*).
Therefore, sin is not supposed to be in our midst (*1 John 2:1*),
and the corporate church should be getting sanctified as a
whole, as each of the parts is individually being sanctified (*2
Corinthians 3:18*). Therefore, we have to take action when one
member is hurting the whole body. The person's sin must
be addressed (*as is indicated Matthew 18:15*). The intent is to
remove the sin (*leaven*) from the midst of the body (*the whole
lump*), which inhibits a Holy God from inhabiting there, and
hurts our ability to dwell in unity with Him (*Psalms 133*).
The idea is **to remove the sin** and any demonic influence
behind it, **not to remove the people.** However, should a
person be unrepentant and unwilling to give up the sin, that
person must be removed from fellowship with the corporate
body in order to get the sin out.

In a like manner, unforgiveness can have very negative consequences in the body. Unforgiveness is divisive and separates brothers from fellowship, limiting their participation and their valuable input into the body. Not only does it hurt the body, but it causes a separation between the person and God. Anything we do to a brother, we do to God since He is also one with that brother, as well as being one with us (*Matthew 25:40*).

Covenant is why Matthew 6:14-15 says that if we don't forgive, we won't be forgiven. When we are alienated from even one friend of His, we are also out of sync with Him. It is only when we make it right and resolve a broken relationship with a friend of God that we can have a restoration of our relationship with Him. Then, we are in good covenant position to receive all the covenant blessings that go with it — including forgiveness. Our fellowship with our brother is closely tied to our fellowship with Him (*1 John 1:7*). Notice in this scripture that our sins are forgiven when we have fellowship with Him **and** our brothers:

> *...but if we walk in the Light as He Himself*
> *is in the Light, we have fellowship with*
> *one another, and the blood of Jesus His*
> *Son cleanses us from all sin.*
>
> *— 1 John 1:7 NASU —*

Even our vision for what the Lord would use us for is closely tied to the vision of the whole body. We cannot walk out our purpose to it's fullest without the wisdom, the assistance, and all the things that the other joints are equipped with to help us develop into a strong kingdom person. At the same time our vision, which is a part of us, is not more important than the corporate body's vision, or the vision of another brother. In fact, if we're going to be faithful (*dead*) covenant people, then our personal vision would not be elevated above anyone else's or above that of the corporate body. In essence, *we die to our own vision to give way for the corporate vision*.

However, *as the corporate vision comes to pass, our individual vision will start to be fulfilled also*. As the church finds it's place in the city and starts to make a favorable impact, we get to function effectively in our part. In essence, the church has a part in the city and we have a part in the church. We are all pieces of the same loaf (*1 Corinthians 10:16*).

There is also an implication that we be the best that we can be. Or stated otherwise, we are to be the best stewards of what the Lord has given us (*1 Peter 4:10*) in order to do what is best not only for us, but also for the corporate body, and for the Lord. In this way we help supply the most and best we can to perfect the outworking of the corporate vision — and enlarge the kingdom. When we function in this way, it enlarges everyone and us as well. This demands that we *continue to grow*, and *continue to be discipled and enlarged* in our ability to *impact the kingdom*.

For though by this time you ought to be teachers, you have need again for someone to teach you the elementary principles of the oracles of God, and you have come to need milk and not solid food. For everyone who partakes only of milk is not accustomed to the word of righteousness, for he is an infant. But solid food is for the mature, who because of practice have their senses trained to discern good and evil.

— Hebrews 5:12-14 NASU —

It isn't necessary for us to be needy all the time. There is a season to grow up and lay down our lives for the body (*to die for, to serve, and to add to the body*). We were not created to remain takers. We were created to mature and become a source of supply for others and not just receive from everyone. When we lay down our lives for the body, we begin to dwell in true unity in the sense that we are committed to their good and not just our own. When we dwell in unity, we are in a sense *"married"* to them, committed to their welfare and their visions. When we dwell in unity we see the anointing and presence of God in our midst, working out of the life that comes forth in our families, impacting our cities, and profoundly changing our world.

How serious does the Lord take all this covenant, oneness, unity stuff? This can best be shown by reviewing what He says in His Word in I Corinthians 11.

> *For as often as you eat this bread and drink the cup, you proclaim the Lord's death until He comes.*
>
> *Therefore whoever eats the bread or drinks the cup of the Lord in an unworthy manner, shall be guilty of the body and the blood of the Lord.*
>
> *But a man must examine himself, and in so doing he is to eat of the bread and drink of the cup.*
>
> *For he who eats and drinks, eats and drinks judgment to himself if he does not judge the body rightly.*

BLOOD COVENANT

For this reason many among you are
weak and sick, and a number sleep.

— *1 Corinthians 11:26-30* NASU —

As often as we take the Lord's Supper, we proclaim that He died *for us all* — His body (*symbolized by the bread*) represents and includes the entire body of Christ that He died for. Therefore, if we commemorate what He did and we are not right with a brother or sister, then we violate the oneness that the bread and the wine stand for. We dishonor Him as well as the ones we have ought against. Remember, what you do to the least, you also do to Him (*Matthew 25:40*).

When we partake of the Lord's Supper while we walk in unforgiveness toward others, we claim His death for us, but not for everyone. This lessens what He did and defiles the table of the Lord. As a result, the covenant blessings and protection are not there for us, and a curse of sickness or death could come upon us because we have violated the terms of the covenant.

To summarize; there are no levels of commitment, covenant means we are *in all the way.* Independent people who refuse to die to self are lukewarm and in danger of being spit from the very mouth of God. We are all one in Christ — each one a member of His body. When we walk in covenant and function in unity, the whole corporate body experiences the benefits and blessings of a covenant relationship with Christ. God cannot dwell with sin, therefore sin must be removed from the body. Walking in covenant with God requires us to walk in forgiveness with our brothers and sisters. Having ought with one of God's friends means that we have ought with God Himself, but when we walk in unity, we have the blessing of the Lord — **"Behold, how good and how pleasant it is for brothers to dwell together in unity!"**

Chapter Four

I'VE GOT YOUR BACK

There is something very secure about the blood covenant relationship — you really know who your friends are. They are loyal, dependable, and can be counted on regardless of the circumstance. They are not just *fair weather* friends, but true friends indeed. In fact, they are closer than your own *blood family*. This is specifically verbalized in the verse below.

A man of too many friends
comes to ruin,

But there is a friend who sticks
closer than a brother.

— Proverbs 18:24 NASU —

One of the issues many people face is, "Who can I really trust?" A covenant friend is your friend as long as he lives. A covenant friend is there for you much like the spouse is to be there for their marriage partner — for better or for worse. All the covenant friend's talents, strengths, and ability to defend or fight are totally at your disposal. In fact, that was one of the motivating factors in making a blood covenant in ancient times — mutual protection. The covenant pact made an adversary think twice about attacking you, as they had to first ascertain who you were in covenant with. Because of the covenant oneness, when one was attacked, it was the same as attacking both.

In other words, what you do to one, you do to the other. That's exactly what the Bible says and means in Matthew 25. Here the Lord actually states that whatever you do to one of His sheep is just like doing it to Him personally:

> *The King will answer and say to them,*
> *"Truly I say to you, to the extent that you*
> *did it to one of these brothers of Mine,*
> *even the least of them, you did it to Me."*

> *— Matthew 25:40 NASU —*

One of the first steps in the ancient ritual of blood covenant was the exchange of the belts and weapons. The belt, which girded a person, symbolized their strength. The weapons attached to the belt symbolized their ability to fight. In essence, the exchange declared, "All your enemies are my enemies and all your friends are my friends (*and vice versa*)." The exhange of belts was also a promise that one's ability to fight or protect were extended to the other one, should any circumstance necessitate it. We see such an exchange actually take place in I Samuel 18 where David and Jonathan make covenant.

> *Now it came about when he had finished*
> *speaking to Saul, that the soul of Jona-*
> *than was knit to the soul of David, and*
> *Jonathan loved him as himself. Saul took*
> *him that day and did not let him return to*
> *his father's house. Then Jonathan made*
> *a covenant with David because he loved*
> *him as himself. Jonathan stripped himself*
> *of the robe that was on him and gave it*

> *to David, with his armor, including his*
> *sword and his bow and his belt.*
>
> *— 1 Samuel 18:1-4 NASU —*

Note that the motivation behind entering into covenant was that they loved each other as themselves — much like the Second Great Commandment (*which is the same covenant commitment we have to each fellow Christian*) found in Matthew 22:39. They were committed to fighting any enemy that was now a mutual enemy — even to the point of death.

In the New Testament we have many passages that reflect the same sentiments regarding both our relationship with God and with each other. We should never be overwhelmed or overrun by circumstances or an attack of the enemy because we have a mighty God and a mighty army of friends who are there for us. No matter how bad the devil may make it look in the natural, we are not without help or hope. Therefore, we can take comfort in the benefits of the covenant.

> *And He has said to me, "My grace is*
> *sufficient for you, for power is perfected*
> *in weakness." Most gladly, therefore, I will*
> *rather boast about my weaknesses, so*
> *that the power of Christ may dwell in me.*
> *Therefore I am well content with weak-*
> *nesses, with insults, with distresses, with*
> *persecutions, with difficulties,*
> *for Christ's sake; for when I am weak,*
> *then I am strong.*
>
> *— 2 Corinthians 12:9-10 NASU —*

We can count on the fact that the battle is the Lord's (1 Samuel 17:47) and that it is not by might or power but by the Spirit (Zechariah 4:6). This means that the Lord may directly open the door to a solution, or fix the problem Himself. He may also do it through the Spirit working through one of our brothers. Either way, we can rest in the covenant assurance that we are not in it alone.

...and that all this assembly may know that the LORD does not deliver by sword or by spear; for the battle is the LORD'S and He will give you into our hands.
— 1 Samuel 17:47 NASU—

Then he said to me, "This is the word of the LORD to Zerubbabel saying, ' Not by might nor by power, but by My Spirit,' says the LORD of hosts."
— Zechariah 4:6 NASU—

In chapter 9 of the book of Joshua, the Israelites have been "on a roll" and they are taking the land of Canaan. The various Canaanite people are very aware of the Israelite presence and many are very fearful, knowing that the God of Israel has given Israel the land (Joshua 2: 9-10).

It is with this backdrop that we see the Gibeonites, who themselves are inhabitants in the land, come on the scene. Here in chapter 9, they deceive Joshua and his leaders, and make them think they came from a far away land. Believing this fabrication, and not inquiring of God, Joshua and the leaders make a covenant with these Gibeonites — a **big** mistake!

There is an unmistakable application here to marriage. The reason for the engagement period is to get to know all about your potential partner. This is not the time to forget about seeking God for his approval of the marriage also. *Many* people rush into marriage and later feel they were deceived or that they should have better understood who the person was they were marrying. Once the honeymoon is over, they feel trapped and find themselves having ought against their partner, feeling an injustice has been perpetrated against them. However, the time to back out was *before* the marriage, now they are in it *for better or for worse*.

Now, back to the book of Joshua, chapter 10. The five kings of the Amorites, who were allies of Gibeon, now see Gibeon as a threat. Gibeon has become an enemy because they are now the covenant friends of Israel. The Amorite kings come together and attack Gibeon. Gibeon, now besieged by their *new* enemies, send word to their *new* friends (*Israel*), asking for help.

Joshua doesn't hesitate to call on God about what he should do. The Lord instructs Joshua to go rescue Gibeon, promising to give the Amorites into his hand. Joshua obeyed, and the scripture indicates that the Lord confounded all the Amorites and slew them with a great slaughter.

In the midst of this battle, God extended the day by causing the sun to stand still and killed even more of the enemy than the Israelites had killed by using hailstones from heaven. This is a great example of what a covenant keeping God will do on behalf of His people — literally, the battle was the Lord's. It was His power and strength that dessimated the enemy.

Notice also what the Lord required of Joshua and Israel. *Even though they had been deceived* into making covenant with Gibeon, Israel *was still obligated* to fight for their new covenant partner. At the same time, the Lord, Himself, went to great lengths to help Israel keep the covenant pact — even using miraculous means to bring victory over the enemy.

God will do the same for the marriage that appears to be on the rocks, as the enemy has both spouses fighting each other (flesh and blood) rather than the real enemy. God will go to great extremes to bring about a victory, even if the marriage got off to a wrong start by one or both partners deceiving each other.

Many in the church are awakening to the existence and need of spiritual warfare, realizing the devil fights dirty. He not only robs, but also wants to destroy and kill (John 10:10). In this spiritual bat-

In Christ we have TOTAL victory!

tle, the Lord has shown Himself strong on our behalf by giving us weapons of warfare that are divinely powerful for pulling down strongholds (2 Corinthians 10:3-5). With His help, we destroy every speculation or lofty thing raised up against the knowledge of God. There is no temptation that is too strong for us, none that He hasn't given us a way out of (1 Corinthians 10:13). When we were weak and helpless (lost), He comes to rescue and deliver. In fact, He has placed at our disposal all He is, and **in Him** (*reference to covenant*) we have total victory.

See to it that no one takes you captive through philosophy and empty deception, according to the tradition of men, according to the elementary principles of the world, rather than according to Christ.

For in Him all the fullness of Deity dwells in bodily form, and in Him you

*have been made complete, and He is the
head over all rule and authority;
and in Him you were also circumcised
with a circumcision made without hands,
in the removal of the body of the flesh by
the circumcision of Christ; having been
buried with Him in baptism, in which you
were also raised up with Him through
faith in the working of God, who raised
Him from the dead.*

*When you were dead in your transgres-
sions and the uncircumcision of your flesh,
He made you alive together with Him,
having forgiven us all our transgressions,
having canceled out the certificate of debt
consisting of decrees against us, which
was hostile to us; and He has taken it out
of the way, having nailed it to the cross.*

*When He had disarmed the rulers
and authorities, He made a public display
of them, having triumphed
over them through Him.*

— Colossians 2:8-15 NASU —

When we put on Christ, we have been armed with spiritual weapons and armor. Then, we are **strong in Him** and
are able to stand against anything the enemy may have up
his sleeve. We each have individual warfare set against us
and our individual purposes. However, we have a covenant
Brother (*Jesus*) who has untold resources and unfathom-

able abilities to cause us to win. The victory is ours because the battle is really His.

Finally, be strong in the Lord and in the strength of His might.
Put on the full armor of God, so that you will be able to stand firm against the schemes of the devil.

For our struggle is not against flesh and blood, but against the rulers, against the powers, against the world forces of this darkness, against the spiritual forces of wickedness in the heavenly places.

Therefore, take up the full armor of God, so that you will be able to resist in the evil day, and having done everything, to stand firm.

Stand firm therefore, HAVING GIRDED YOUR LOINS WITH TRUTH, and HAVING PUT ON THE BREASTPLATE OF RIGHTEOUSNESS, and having shod YOUR FEET WITH THE PREPARATION OF THE GOSPEL OF PEACE; in addition to all, taking up the shield of faith with which you will be able to extinguish all the flaming arrows of the evil one.

And take THE HELMET OF SALVATION, and the sword of the Spirit, which is the word of God.

— Ephesians 6:10-17 NASU —

One of our greatest weapons is the Word of God. The devil hates the Word because it exposes his schemes and who he is. This powerful weapon should be used as Jesus used it against the devil when He was in the wilderness (Matthew 4:1-11). The Word of God cuts through all the lies and any confusion, going right to the heart of any matter.

For the word of God is living and active
and sharper than any two-edged sword,
and piercing as far as the division of soul
and spirit, of both joints and marrow,
and able to judge the thoughts and
intentions of the heart.

— Hebrews 4:12 NASU —

We are not in the battle alone. We have many Christian brothers and sisters going through their own spiritual battles. We need each other. We need to intercede and pray for one another. This is not something that is just a nice thing to do — it is a covenant *obligation*. We need to use everything we have at our disposal to restore a fellow Christian who is being beat up or held captive by the enemy. After all, that's what Jesus came to do, and we are challenged to do the same:

The Spirit of the Lord GOD is upon me,
Because the LORD has anointed me
To bring good news to the afflicted;
He has sent me to bind up the
brokenhearted,
To proclaim liberty to captives
And freedom to prisoners;

BLOOD COVENANT

To proclaim the favorable year
of the LORD
And the day of vengeance of our God;
To comfort all who mourn,
To grant those who mourn in Zion,
Giving them a garland instead of ashes,
The oil of gladness instead of mourning,
The mantle of praise instead of
a spirit of fainting.
So they will be called oaks
of righteousness,
The planting of the LORD,
that He may be glorified.
— Isaiah 61:1-3 NASU —

This is exactly what is also recorded in Luke 4:18 in the New Testament. This is not just an instruction, but a covenant requirement. We are to meet needs and fight battles that would assist others in getting free from their oppression and bondage. This is how we demonstrate our love — we love them as ourselves, and this love will **cover a multitude of sins** (1 Peter 4:7).

My brethren, if any among you strays
from the truth and one turns him back,
let him know that he who turns
a sinner from the error of his way will
save his soul from death
and will cover a multitude of sins.

— James 5:19-20 NASU —

Intercession is one way we can (and should) help a brother in need. Warring against the devil, quoting the Word of God, praying prophetically, and rebuking in the Name of Jesus should be normal. In fact, they should be automatic reactions whenever we find someone in a test, trial, temptation, or whatever else they may be fighting. We should fight the battle through to the end. That's why good intercessors *pray through* a situation, continuing to intercede until they feel the issue has been dealt with and the person they have been praying for is 'over the hump.'

We need to be careful, to be good covenant people in right standing before our Lord, choosing the things of the Spirit and not of the flesh. We are warned in the book of James that if we are in covenant with Him, we will not embrace the things of the world; or we will be adulterers.

You adulteresses, do you not know
that friendship with the world
is hostility toward God?

Therefore, whoever wishes to be a friend of
the world makes himself an enemy of God.

Or do you think that the Scripture speaks
to no purpose: "He jealously desires the
Spirit which He has made to dwell in us?"

But He gives a greater grace.
Therefore it says, "GOD IS OPPOSED
TO THE PROUD, BUT GIVES
GRACE TO THE HUMBLE."

Submit therefore to God.
Resist the devil and he will flee from you.

BLOOD COVENANT

*Draw near to God and He will
draw near to you.*

— James 4:3-9 NASU —

It is when we become friends with God's enemy that we are seen as His enemies. In our rebellion we are not in good covenant standing. It is then that we don't have His strength or abilities to fight our battles. It is when we come back into agreement (*become good covenant friends*) that we have the grace to resist the devil and win in the battle. It is when we are again in good covenant standing that we will see the power of God move in our behalf. We will be **strong in the Lord** and **see the enemy flee**, as our prayers are more effective (James 5:16) and we can totally rely on the armor of God.

There is no greater ally than God. There is no greater friend and no more terrifying enemy. When you understand the power and protection that comes from walking in blood covenant with God, you can live free from fear and walk in boldness knowing that God has your back!

Chapter Five

DEAD MEN WALKING

The biggest issue faced when trying to walk in covenant, whether it be in relation to our earthly friends or to God, is dying to ourselves. Dying to self is tough, and the devil is working overtime to keep our flesh alive. His strategy is to keep us focused on the natural and remain overly sensitive to the words and actions of those around us. In that way, we easily become offended and our instinct is to preserve self. Offense causes us to pull back from others so we are not in fellowship with everyone in the light. The trouble is that when we do this, *we* are *also* not in the light (in fellowship) with Christ either! What we do to a brother or sister in Christ — we do to Him (Matthew 25:40).

If someone says, "I love God," and hates his brother, he is a liar; for the one who does not love his brother whom he has seen, cannot love God whom he has not seen. And this commandment we have from Him, that the one who loves God should love his brother also.

—1 John 4:19-21 NASU —

> *...but if we walk in the Light as He Himself
> is in the Light, we have fellowship with
> one another, and the blood of Jesus His
> Son cleanses us from all sin.*

> *— 1 John 1:7 NASU —*

In the ancient ritual of blood covenant, the two making covenant walk between the pieces of the animal that has been cut in half. This walk is called the **walk of death**. This signifies a dying to who I am and a total commitment to my new covenant friend. The death to self of each individual is a vital part of covenant. Without it, the covenant would not be effective and function as it was designed to function.

> *For where a covenant is, there must of
> necessity be the death of the one who
> made it. For a covenant is valid only when
> men are dead, for it is never in force while
> the one who made it lives.*

> *— Hebrews 9:16-17 NASU —*

As we have seen, dying to self is crucial if we are going to be faithful covenant people. The Apostle Paul says in First Corinthians that he dies daily. This is not a paradox, but rather an indication that Paul's old nature rises up within him, and each day, he must make a conscious decision to crucify his flesh and die to self in order that he might live in Christ.

*I affirm, brethren, by the boasting
in you which I have in Christ Jesus
our Lord, I die daily.*

— *1 Corinthians 15:31* NASU —

While this statement may seem extreme, it is the exact formula we must follow. The death talked about here is a process, a daily walk of repentance. This involves changing everything — thought patterns, habits, attitudes, words, etc. Anything that does not match the holy standard we are expected to walk in must be changed. This is the good work He will complete until the day of salvation (Philippians 1:6). Step by step, as the Holy Spirit teaches us, we yield to His desires and sin *less* on the road to *sinlessness*.

*But we all, with unveiled face,
beholding as in a mirror the glory of
the Lord, are being transformed into
the same image from glory to glory,
just as from the Lord, the Spirit.*

— *2 Corinthians 3:18* NASU —

This verse shows us beyond question that we are to be led by the Spirit. The same Holy Spirit that raised Jesus from the dead is quickening our mortal bodies. As a result, we are walking above the worldly temptations and entanglements — as a stranger in an alien land (Hebrews 11:9). In so doing, we are the friends of God and not friends of the world (James 4:4).

*But if the Spirit of Him who raised Jesus
from the dead dwells in you, He who
raised Christ Jesus from the dead will also
give life to your mortal bodies through
His Spirit who dwells in you.*

*So then, brethren, we are under obliga-
tion, not to the flesh, to live according to
the flesh — for if you are living according
to the flesh, you must die; but if by the
Spirit you are putting to death the deeds
of the body, you will live.*

*For all who are being led by the Spirit of
God, these are sons of God.*

— Romans 8:11-14 NASU —

Water Baptism

Dying is a choice that we, like Paul, have to choose
every day (Deuteronomy 30:19-20). We begin this process
of dying the very moment we enter the kingdom of God,
with water baptism being a critical step. So critical that
it is a command — much more than a symbolic gesture
or hollow ritual.

*What shall we say then? Are we to continue
in sin so that grace may increase?*

*May it never be! How shall we who died to
sin still live in it?*

Or do you not know that all of us who have been baptized into Christ Jesus have been baptized into His death?

Therefore we have been buried with Him through baptism into death, so that as Christ was raised from the dead through the glory of the Father, so we too might walk in newness of life.

For if we have become united with Him in the likeness of His death, certainly we shall also be in the likeness of His resurrection, knowing this, that our old self was crucified with Him, in order that our body of sin might be done away with, so that we would no longer be slaves to sin; for he who has died is freed from sin.

Now if we have died with Christ, we believe that we shall also live with Him, knowing that Christ, having been raised from the dead, is never to die again; death no longer is master over Him.

For the death that He died, He died to sin once for all; but the life that He lives, He lives to God.

Even so consider yourselves to be dead to sin, but alive to God in Christ Jesus.

Therefore do not let sin reign in your mortal body so that you obey its lusts, and do not go on presenting the members of your body to sin as instruments of unrighteousness; but present yourselves to God as those alive from the dead, and your members as instruments of righteousness to God.

For sin shall not be master over you, for you are not under law but under grace.

What then? Shall we sin because we are not under law but under grace? May it never be!

Do you not know that when you present yourselves to someone as slaves for obedience, you are slaves of the one whom you obey, either of sin resulting in death, or of obedience resulting in righteousness?

But thanks be to God that though you were slaves of sin, you became obedient from the heart to that form of teaching to which you were committed, and having been freed from sin, you became slaves of righteousness.

— Romans 6:1-18 NASU —

So, when we go into the baptism waters, we have died legally. When we rise from the waters of baptism, we rise with the ability to choose life and not death. We are **no** *longer slaves to sin,* but instead are to submit our bodies to Him as a sacrifice — now a slave to righteousness. In this, baptism is the equivalent of the Old Testament circumcision. In the Old Testament, this was a literal cutting away of flesh, but in baptism it is a cutting away of the old sin nature — it is a circumcision of the heart. Obedience in baptism allows us to choose to walk in true covenant "deadness."

> *...and in Him you were also circumcised with **a circumcision made without hands**, in the removal of the body of the flesh by the circumcision of Christ; having been buried with Him in baptism, in which you were also raised up with Him through faith in the working of God, who raised Him from the dead.*
>
> *— Colossians 2:11-12 NASU —*

Seek First The Kingdom

While on earth, the Lord was very specific about what constituted dying to ourselves. It is really dying to all that's in the world except Him. That's what it means in Matthew 6:33 when it states we are to seek the kingdom first, along with righteousness. These should be our goals above all else — above our ministries, our family, our finances and all our possessions. When considering the First Great Commandment (which is really a covenant commitment), this makes perfect sense.

*And He said to him, "YOU SHALL LOVE
THE LORD YOUR GOD WITH ALL
YOUR HEART, AND WITH ALL YOUR
SOUL, AND WITH ALL YOUR MIND."*

— *Matthew 22:37 NASU* —

When you follow the words of Jesus in regards to being His disciple, the way ***is narrow.*** You are walking in covenant oneness with Him. In Luke 14:26, He addresses His stance on the family issue, which shouldn't be surprising considering Proverbs indicates the covenant brother is closer than a family member (Proverbs 18:24).

Who Is My Family?

*If anyone comes to Me, and does not
hate his own father and mother
and wife and children and brothers and
sisters, yes, and even his own life,
he cannot be My disciple.*

— *Luke 14:26 NASU* —

This is further validated in the Gospels, both in Mark and Luke, when the crowds refer to Jesus' natural family. Jesus uses these opportunities to express His thoughts regarding who He saw as His family. This is offensive to some. It seems cold toward his own natural relatives, related by geneology, and shows a preference for those with whom He is in covenant.

*But He answered and said to them, "My
mother and My brothers are these who
hear the word of God and do it."*

— *Luke 8:21 NASU* —

Looking about at those who were sitting around Him, He said, " Behold My mother and My brothers!

— Mark 3:34 NASU —

You have heard the saying, "*blood is thicker than water.*" Through the eyes of Western culture, we understand this to mean that the ties with our natural family are a stronger bond than ties with "*outsiders.*" This phrase has been the excuse for family feuds carried on for generations. In fact, the origination of this phrase is found deep in the Arab culture, and is still in use today. The original phrase is, "*blood is thicker than milk.*" It is not meant to defend ties to family members. On the contrary, it is meant to describe the strength of a blood covenant bond. The reference to milk is mother's milk and indicates that the tie to the blood brother is stronger than the tie one's own mother — natural relatives. Jesus made it clear that His true family was made up of those in blood covenant with Him.

Possessions

He doesn't stop there, Jesus also doesn't hold back on the subject of possessions. He and His kingdom come first, regardless! Nothing should stand in the way of the covenant relationship He wants to have with us.

So then, none of you can be My disciple who does not give up all his own possessions.

— Luke 14:33 NASU —

This does not mean that we are all to take up a vow of poverty and live in the back side of the desert. Much like what was spoken and implied to the rich young ruler, this is speaking to an issue of the heart. Money or possessions are not a problem, as long as you are not more attached to them than you are to the Lord.

> *For the love of money is a root of all sorts of evil, and some by longing for it have wandered away from the faith and pierced themselves with many griefs.*
>
> — *1 Timothy 6:10 NASU* —

Notice that this addresses and speaks against the **love of money**, as opposed to money itself. This is because money is amoral. It is neither good nor bad. Money is not evil unless we let it turn our heart away from the Lord in favor of it and what it can buy and influence.

The Second Great Commandment

The Second Great Commandment is really a covenant statement regarding our brothers and sisters in Christ. It shows we are all equal before Him and should love each other even as ourself (since we are also a good creation of His). We are not to be partial or prejudiced, and if we really love them, we will serve them all, and meet their needs.

> *The second is like it, "YOU SHALL LOVE YOUR NEIGHBOR AS YOURSELF."*
>
> — *Matthew 22:39 NASU* —

This being the case, we would be willing to set aside our agendas, our preferences, and allot the time, abilities, even finances to aid or assist the ones we love as much as we do ourselves. In fact, the Bible implies we should even prefer them.

Therefore if there is any encouragement in Christ, if there is any consolation of love, if there is any fellowship of the Spirit, if any affection and compassion, make my joy complete by being of the same mind, maintaining the same love, united in spirit, intent on one purpose.

Do nothing from selfishness or empty conceit, but with humility of mind regard one another as more important than yourselves; do not merely look out for your own personal interests, but also for the interests of others.

— Philippians 2:1-4 NASU —

If we are truly in covenant, then we would even be willing to lay down our lives for the brethren. This doesn't just mean we would be willing to *"take a bullet"* for them in the right circumstance. It means that we must die to our lives and needs, and be willing to help or serve them when there is a problem or a need.

We know that we have passed out of death into life, because we love the brethren. He who does not love abides in death.

Everyone who hates his brother is a murderer; and you know that no murderer has eternal life abiding in him.

*We know love by this, that He laid down
His life for us; and we ought to lay down
our lives for the brethren.*

*But whoever has the world's goods, and
sees his brother in need and closes his
heart against him, how does the
love of God abide in him?*

*Little children, let us not love with word
or with tongue, but in deed and truth.*

— *1 John 3:14-18* NASU —

Money is a real dividing line. Many people are willing to help another with an encouraging word, a prayer or a bit of advice, but they are a little *"tight"* or hesitant to meet a financial need. Money is not the most important ingredient as far as fulfilling covenant requirements, but money is a true indicator of the heart. Does not the Bible say that where your treasure is, there your heart is also (Matt 6:19-21)? In the context of our discussion, this means that if you withhold financially from your brother who has a genuine need (*when you are in a position to help*), you really don't love him and are not a true covenant person.

Corporate Vision

We all need to have vision. It is vital to every individual to understand our individual purposes and walk in our destiny. However, our purpose, or any vision God has given us, doesn't trump someone else's vision. Again, we are to be covenant people willing to prefer our covenant brother. In this context, we need to *"die"* to our vision for the sake of the corporate body, that is the church or ministry or group you are a committed part of. Let's use the church as an example.

There should be a city or regional vision for your area — and one that is unselfish, one that elevates the kingdom and the Body of Christ — not specific to any one single church. Pastors and individual church members must lay down their personal visions, giving preference to the vision for the city (or region). When there is unity in the body and all are working toward common vision, as the city/regional vision comes to pass, the churches will find themselves fulfilling their corporate visions in support of the city. Each church helps frame the vision and each individual member holds a vital piece of the larger picture.

Likewise, as the church vision unfolds, the personal visions will also come to pass, as the individuals will be a part of what the church is doing. So, through our covenant unity, there will be a realization of the blessing of life (Psalm 133:3) over our lives, our church and our city.

One thing will be evident when we die to ourselves. Much like what happens in the waters of baptism, if we die with Him, we will be raised to newness of life. So it will be in our families, in our relationships, in our churches, and in our cities. Our death precipitates a resurrection, a newness, a freshness that benefits the corporate group as well as ourselves. We will realize life — and life more abundantly! The world will be drawn by the covenant unity (*love*) we have for one another.

This death also opens the door to the power of God working in us and through us. In Acts 1:8, Jesus tells the disciples to remain in Jerusalem until they receive the power from the Holy Spirit. Then, they would become the witnesses He wanted in the world. However, the word *witness* means *martyr*, which implies that one of the main characteristic of a true witness is that they are "*dead.*" It

71

can be implied that we need to decrease *(die)* so He can increase *(in power)* within us, so we can better represent Him. We are to be dead men walking.

...but you will receive power when the Holy Spirit has come upon you; and you shall be My witnesses both in Jerusalem, and in all Judea and Samaria, and even to the remotest part of the earth.

— Acts 1:8 NASU —

Chapter Six

FAITHFULNESS IS BLESSED, DISOBEDIENCE IS NOT

Faithfulness is defined as being trustworthy; steady; firm; loyal; steadfast in keeping promises or in fulfilling duties. This definition is agreed upon by both the concordance and the dictionary. To be found faithful requires an unfailing level of commitment. Faithfulness involves loyalty that transcends our comfort or preference. This sounds remarkably like a covenant commitment — which biblical faithfulness implies.

Faithfulness suggests an unwavering position; being firm in your resolve. This is something that cannot be done by yourself, but only through the grace of God (2 Corinthians 12:9-10). A good illustration of this is building your house on the rock. We are not to be moved or shaken by all the forces (*resistance*) that the enemy brings against us. Instead we are to remain faithful (*solid*), no matter what.

We are to remain faithful to the Lord and to our brothers in Christ. This is a result of a genuine dying love for both.

Therefore everyone who hears these
words of Mine and acts on them,
may be compared to a wise man
who built his house on the rock.
And the rain fell, and the floods came,
and the winds blew and slammed against
that house; and yet it did not fall, for it
had been founded on the rock. Everyone
who hears these words of Mine and does
not act on them, will be like a foolish man
who built his house on the sand. The rain
fell, and the floods came, and the winds
blew and slammed against that house;
and it fell — and great was its fall.
— Matthew 7:24-27 NASU —

Faithfulness is an important covenant issue. Faithfulness is an important covenant issue. When one takes covenant vows they are bound to be faithful to the vows, and thereby faithful to their covenant friends. Marriage is a good example. The marriage vows may vary in any given ceremony, based on the word preference of those getting married. However, the wording should all specify or imply that the covenant is irrevocable and is unto death. Remember, a covenant is only valid when men are dead (*to themselves*).

For where a covenant is, there must of necessity be the death of the one who made it. **For a covenant is valid only when men are dead,** *for it is never in force while the one who made it lives*

— Hebrews 9:16-17 NASU —

There is a trend in modern culture to *water down* the marriage vows. This is an attempt by some to become more relevant to today's culture. What it really means is becoming more politically correct. Any wording that indicates commitment is purposely avoided so that people aren't bound or tied down — remaining free to be who they are. How much weight does a marriage vow have when a prenuptial agreement has been signed to cover an eventual divorce? I mentioned earlier that there is even a tendency for the *modern woman* to retain her maiden name! This is done so she won't be swallowed up by or be hidden in the shadow of her husband — a total misunderstanding of covenant.

This tragedy is a direct result of the impact world culture has on the church. Covenant by its very nature *demands* commitment (*i.e., faithfulness*), something that many people avoid today like a plague. There is a fear that any commitment will hinder them from being who they are and doing what they want — **and they are right**! They want it to be all about them at the expense of others. Covenant is all about others at the expense of self.

An example of this is seen by the increase in the number of people who "*live together*" rather than risk the commitment of entering into the marriage covenant. It's much like what is written in the book of Isaiah in the Old Testament.

*For seven women will take hold of one
man in that day, saying, "We will eat our
own bread and wear our own clothes,
only let us be called by your name;
take away our reproach!"*

— *Isaiah 4:1* NASU —

Here, as mentioned before, is the perfect example of **un-faithful** people wanting to do their own thing. They are not willing to give up anything, but still want all the benefits of covenant living. They are totally alive to themselves. They are living, looking for their blessing, because that's what they think it's all about. They refuse to give themselves away and commit to others (we will *wear our own clothes*), but want all the covenant benefits (*let us be called by your name, and take away our reproach*). This is similar to what we see the Bible says in the book of James.

*You ask and do not receive, because
you ask with wrong motives, so that you
may spend it on your pleasures. You
adulteresses, do you not know
that friendship with the world is
hostility toward God? Therefore whoever
wishes to be a friend of the world
makes himself an enemy of God.*

— *James 4:3-4* NASU —

The implication here is clear. The ones he is writing to are worldly, choosing only what they want or want to do (eat my own bread), rather than shunning them for the things of God. They are spiritual adulterers — not faithfully committed to the Lord's covenant. They have chosen not to be faithful to the Lord, but to be *friends* with the *world*. In the book of Hosea it is worded even more strongly. It calls such people harlots (*prostitutes*) because they forsake the Lord for another friend.

When the LORD first spoke through Hosea, the LORD said to Hosea, "Go, take to yourself a wife of harlotry and have children of harlotry; for the land commits flagrant harlotry, forsaking the LORD."
— Hosea 1:2 NASU —

We are the ones who decide whether our lives will be characterized by life or death, by blessings or curses. When we walk as faithful covenant people, we are obedient and submitted to the Lord, and we are in proper fellowship with our brothers — we abide in Him (1 John 3:24). Those who abide in Him are assured of His favor and blessings. This is seen in the ancient ritual of making the blood covenant. The participants pronounced blessings over each other for keeping covenant, as well as curses for not keeping covenant.

I call heaven and earth to witness against you today, that I have set before you life and death, the blessing and the curse.

*So choose life in order that you may live,
you and your descendants, by loving the
LORD your God, by obeying His voice,
and by holding fast to Him; for this is
your life and the length of your days,
that you may live in the land which the
LORD swore to your fathers, to Abraham,
Isaac, and Jacob, to give them."*

— Deuteronomy 30: 19-20 NASU —

Holding fast to Him would include holding fast to His word, whether it be in written form (*Bible*), or by a spoken word (*prophecy, wise counsel, etc*). He and His word are the same (John 1:1) and He watches over His word to perform it (Jeremiah 1:12). Blessings and success are therefore tied to our embracing His word, that is, abiding in Him. When we abide in Him, we are in good covenant standing and in the position to receive all covenant blessings that would be coming our way — *including* prospering in every way.

*How blessed is the man who does not
walk in the counsel of the wicked, Nor
stand in the path of sinners, Nor sit in
the seat of scoffers! But his delight is in
the law of the LORD, And in His law he
meditates day and night. He will be like
a tree firmly planted by streams of water,
Which yields its fruit in its season
And its leaf does not wither;
And in whatever he does, he prospers.*

*The wicked are not so, But they are
like chaff which the wind drives away.
Therefore the wicked will not stand in the
judgment, Nor sinners in the assembly of
the righteous. For the LORD knows the
way of the righteous, But the way of the
wicked will perish.*

— Psalms 1:1-6 NASU —

Notice that there is a penalty for not walking upright or in accordance with His word. When we are out of covenant, we are out of His will and out from under His protection. Instead of having a righteous walk, we will have an unrighteous (*wicked*) walk. The end result is the disfavor of the Lord and the curses that accompany disobedience. The wages of sin is death (Romans 6:23) — this is a covenant passage from the New Testament that expresses the outcome of not walking a faithful covenant walk.

This is further substantiated by a passage in the book of James, where blessing and obedience are directly linked. We either abide in His word **or** we are forgetful hearers. It is by the obedient doing of the word that we prove our faithfulness, acknowledge His Lordship in our lives, and take our proper covenant position – **and** are blessed. If we don't obey, we are deluded (James 1:22).

*But one who looks intently at the perfect
law, the law of liberty, and abides by it,
not having become a forgetful hearer
but an effectual doer, this man will
be blessed in what he does.*

— James 1:25 NASU —

It follows that being faithful is a measure by which God can determine your kingdom usefulness — gauging if He can really trust you. Once this is established, He can bring you into bigger and better things *including* more blessing! So covenant faithfulness is a prerequisite to continuing in His work and favor, *especially* the handling of finances!

He who is faithful in a very little thing is faithful also in much; and he who is unrighteous in a very little thing is unrighteous also in much. Therefore if you have not been faithful in the use of unrighteous wealth, who will entrust the true riches to you? And if you have not been faithful in the use of that which is another's, who will give you that which is your own? No servant can serve two masters; for either he will hate the one and love the other, or else he will be devoted to one and despise the other. You cannot serve God and wealth.

— Luke 16:10-13 NASU —

We see here that good stewardship in all areas is a covenant issue. We come into this world naked and go out the same way (Job 1:21). Everything we have is given by the Lord for a kingdom purpose, either to sustain us or to invest in others (1 John 3:16-17, 1 Timothy 6:17-19). Our faithfulness in properly using these resources is an issue of covenantal obedience. This applies to money, especially, since it is the one thing that is prone to turn men's hearts from God to chase the things of the world (1 Timothy 6:10, Matthew 6:24).

When Jesus sent out the twelve in the book of Matthew, He told them to teach and do kingdom things (Matthew 10:7-8). The things you receive, you are to turn around and use to serve or give to others — meeting needs, helping the hurting and downtrodden. It is also properly utilizing what the gifts and talents were for. They are kingdom resources that are meant to be used for blessing others. That's why Jesus said "freely you receive, freely you give."

The same is true of all gifts. They are covenant gifts. In effect, "All I have is yours." That is why it states in 1 Corinthians 12:7 that the gifts are for the common good. That is why we are enjoined in 1 Peter — to be good covenant stewards of all the grace we have received.

As each one has received a special gift, employ it in serving one another as good stewards of the manifold grace of God.

— 1 Peter 4:10 NASU —

When we are faithful and abiding in His covenant, we will absolutely not go without due reward. That is part of His faithfulness, not only to His word, but also to us. That's what sowing and reaping are all about.

Do not be deceived, God is not mocked; for whatever a man sows, this he will also reap. For the one who sows to his own flesh will from the flesh reap corruption, but the one who sows to the Spirit will from the Spirit reap eternal life.

BLOOD COVENANT

*Let us not lose heart in doing good, for
in due time we will reap if we do not
grow weary. So then, while we have opportunity, let us do good to all people,
and especially to those who are of the
household of the faith.*

— *Galatians 6:7-10 NASU* —

We see in this passage, that it is not about us and our
flesh, it is about the Spirit, the kingdom, and the bond
of unity we have with our Christian brothers. While we
bless, meet needs, encourage, and edify our
brothers, we are being faithful to them
and to the Lord. We are thereby good
covenant partners. In so doing, we are
in line for all the covenant blessings
that accrue.

*It is not
about us —
it is about
the Spirit!*

We have already discussed the fact
that there were blessings for keeping cov-
enant and curses for breaking covenant. This is specifically
outlined in Deuteronomy 28 where we see the blessings
and curses that are enumerated in the Old Testament for
keeping covenant (*being obedient —Deut. 28:1-14*) or breaking covenant (*being disobedient—Deut. 28:15-68*).

Faithfulness brings blessing. You will not fail to receive
these rewards if you remain faithful. Do not grow weary
in being a good covenant partner. Deuteronomy 28:2 says
that these blessings will actually **overtake** you. In other
words, there is no way that you will miss them, if you are
due them. As an example, read the list of blessings in the
scripture that follows.

FAITHFULNESS IS BLESSED...

Now it shall be, if you diligently obey the LORD your God, being careful to do all His commandments which I command you today, the LORD your God will set you high above all the nations of the earth.

All these blessings will come upon you and overtake you if you obey the LORD your God:

Blessed shall you be in the city, and blessed shall you be in the country.

Blessed shall be the offspring of your body and the produce of your ground and the offspring of your beasts, the increase of your herd and the young of your flock.

Blessed shall be your basket and your kneading bowl.

Blessed shall you be when you come in, and blessed shall you be when you go out.

The LORD shall cause your enemies who rise up against you to be defeated before you; they will come out against you one way and will flee before you seven ways.

The LORD will command the blessing upon you in your barns and in all that you put your hand to, and He will bless you in the land which the LORD your God gives you.

BLOOD COVENANT

The LORD will establish you as a holy people to Himself, as He swore to you, if you keep the commandments of the LORD your God and walk in His ways.

So all the peoples of the earth will see that you are called by the name of the LORD, and they will be afraid of you.

The LORD will make you abound in prosperity, in the offspring of your body and in the offspring of your beast and in the produce of your ground, in the land which the LORD swore to your fathers to give you.

The LORD will open for you His good storehouse, the heavens, to give rain to your land in its season and to bless all the work of your hand; and you shall lend to many nations, but you shall not borrow.

The LORD will make you the head and not the tail, and you only will be above, and you will not be underneath, if you listen to the commandments of the LORD your God, which I charge you today, to observe them carefully, and do not turn aside from any of the words which I command you today, to the right or to the left, to go after other gods to serve them.
— Deuteronomy 28:1-14 NASU —

We can easily see that faithfulness is a paramount issue with the Lord. We must prove faithful in all areas of our lives if we are to be blessed and if we are to be proper examples for those who will follow us. It is through our faithfulness that there will be no dilution of His word and no abuse in the use of the gifts of the Holy Spirit.

The Lord wants to use faithful people because they are the ones committed and loyal to Him, to His kingdom, and to His people. We are to think as He thinks and be careful with whom we entrust the things of the kingdom. Paul instructs Timothy to pass on what he has *only to faithful men* who in turn will be good stewards in handling kingdom things — no pearls given to swine. So, part of our faithfulness is to protect the things of God. We are to ensure they will continue to be properly handled, as we disciple those who will be here long after we depart. This will ensure covenant truth, obedience and unity will remain in tact long after we are gone.

The things, which you have heard from me in the presence of many witnesses, entrust these to faithful men who will be able to teach others also.

— 2 Timothy 2:2 NASU —

In summation, we now understand that obedience (from the heart) equates to covenant faithfulness. This in turn ensures that we are abiding in Him (in good covenant standing) which brings the Lord's grace, favor and prosperity (covenant blessings) to our lives. So, to some extent we are in control of the outcomes in our life. It is not mere chance or circumstance that dictates our fate. We *choose* life or death, blessings or curses, through our daily decisions to follow (or not to follow) the Lord's directions and commands.

Your faithfulness makes you trustworthy to God.

-Edwin Louis Cole

Chapter Seven

YOUR SPOUSE — YOUR COVENANT FRIEND

Does the title of this chapter sound a little strange? Remember, friend is a covenant term. Therefore, when you enter marriage, your spouse becomes your covenant friend and is now closer to you than a brother (Proverbs 18:24).

Marriage is a blood covenant. All the principles of blood covenant that we have addressed, also apply to marriage. In fact, I have (*jokingly*) said that the marriage ceremony is really a double funeral. Why? Because both parties are committing to die to themselves so they can live for each other and their new union. Entering the marriage covenant brings death to their old life as they move into a completely new life.

There are many traditions and cultural practices surrounding a wedding ceremony that have their origins firmly rooted in the ancient ritual of blood covenant. So, even though the ceremony may seem nice and sweet, there is a deep, serious, covenant basis for most of what is done.

To begin, there is a unique oneness (*unity*) or bond established, *especially* once the marriage is consummated. Genesis 2:24 and Ephesians 5:31 both refer to this oneness.

It is a bond that is not to be broken, but is to be in force until death separates the partners. This, if you remember, is implied in the walk of death — the covenant walk through the pieces of the split animal. This is also signified by the inseparable oneness described in the prophetic gestures of the clasping of wrists and the feeding of the bread and wine to each other in the memorial meal. In fact, the Lord specifically states that this joining together in covenant is a bond that is not to be broken (*divorce*).

> *Some Pharisees came to Jesus, testing Him and asking, "Is it lawful for a man to divorce his wife for any reason at all?" And He answered and said, "Have you not read that He who created them from the beginning MADE THEM MALE AND FEMALE, and said, 'FOR THIS REASON A MAN SHALL LEAVE HIS FATHER AND MOTHER AND BE JOINED TO HIS WIFE, AND THE TWO SHALL BECOME ONE FLESH'? So they are no longer two, but one flesh. What therefore God has joined together, let no man separate."*

Matthew 19:3-7 NASU

This oneness is also termed a **soul tie**. A soul tie can take place between any two people where there is sexual involvement. As a result, we can tie ourselves to a number of partners through immoral behavior. It is incumbent upon us to have any of these immoral soul ties broken before entering marriage. This is important so that we are tied in this special way **only to our spouse**.

Or do you not know that the one who joins himself to a prostitute is one body with her? For He says, "THE TWO SHALL BECOME ONE FLESH."

1 Corinthians 6:16 NASU

Unfaithfulness (*adultery*) in the marriage is a covenant breaking issue by which one partner violates the marriage covenant and legitimizes a separation (Matthew 19:9). The Bible says this is akin to us choosing or attaching ourselves (*joining ourselves*) to money or anything of the world, which is a forsaking of God. The Lord Himself calls it adultery.

You adulteresses, do you not know that friendship with the world is hostility toward God? Therefore whoever wishes to be a friend of the world makes himself an enemy of God.

James 4:4 NASU

The marriage ceremony is performed before witnesses just as the blood covenant ritual was. There is the exchange of vows before God and witnesses, which is a formal commitment to one another as long as they both shall live. Another common practice at the modern day wedding reception is when the new partners feed each other wedding cake. This comes directly from the covenant meal that was taken between two people when making a blood covenant. They fed each other bread dipped in wine, indicating that, "Into me I take you," and vice versa.

The wife commonly takes the husbands name — she goes *into* the name of her new husband much like we go *into* the Name of our Husband (*Christ*) at water baptism. We have a new identity as a result of being tied to our partner and all they have is ours and all that is ours is now theirs.

There is an exchange of rings, and they are intended to be worn (*displayed*) from then on. This is a picture of the blood covenant scars that occurred from the cutting of the wrists so the blood could flow into each other's bodies. This signified an inseparable oneness. Like the scars, the rings are permanent reminders (*signs*) to us and others that we are permanently bound in covenant to a marriage partner.

Once the covenant vows are made, we cannot back out, even if we feel we were deceived or that we made a bad mistake. That's why engagement periods are so important. It is during this time that we really have the opportunity to get to know the person. We must know to whom we are giving ourselves away for the rest of our lives. After marriage it is too late to turn around and go back. The vows are **until death do us part!**

A good picture of this takes place in the book of Joshua, chapters 9 and 10. Here we see Joshua and Israel deceived by the Gibeonites. These were Canaanite inhabitants who realized Israel was going to annihilate all the Canaanite peoples and, out of survival, lied and manipulated Israel into making covenant with them. Once in covenant with Gibeon, Israel couldn't kill them and was "stuck" living with them.

We learn in chapter ten that the five kings of the Amorites (*who were formerly friends of Gibeon*), are now their enemies as a result of this covenant made with Israel. They therefore attack Gibeon, which was in no position to survive such an onslaught. Then, Gibeon appeals to their new "friends" Israel for help.

Joshua inquires of God what to do. God tells him to defend Gibeon and here is where the story (*history*) gets very interesting. In the ensuing battle, God goes to miraculous means to help Joshua defend his covenant partners from enemy attack. He even stops the sun to increase the hours of daylight, and at the same time, slays more Amorites using hailstones from heaven than the Israelites kill.

The moral of the story is this: God is a covenant God and wants us to be a covenant people. Even after being deceived into covenant, He expects us to remain faithful to our commitment (*covenant/marriage vows*). He will go to great extremes to help us keep covenant and even help us defeat all enemies that would try to break up the covenant.

So, once committed by the marriage vows, we are obligated to continue as faithful covenant partners. Everything is part of the oneness and is to be held in common (*such as money, property, and all other assets—there were no prenuptial agreements in the Bible*). Even our bodies are no longer our own (1 Corinthians 7:1-5). We are to be dead to ourselves and alive to our partner. We are obligated to meet their needs and die to ourselves and our preferences.

There is also the requirement to remain *dead*, for a covenant walk is a walk of repentance. We have to keep ourselves active in a dying process — *dying daily (1 Corinthians 15:31)* so we will remain a faithful covenant person (*marriage partner*). The devil hates covenant. He particularly despises the marriage covenant, because the oneness and the synergy that results is a threat to his kingdom.

Remaining dead to self is difficult. We are not to **come alive** to ourselves and judge our partners (Ephesians 6:12). Instead we are to forgive them for any thoughtless, or potentially wounding behavior. In this way also, we are being faithful to our vows and we will keep our hearts right with our marriage partner. If we are unable to do this, we *come alive* in our flesh, find ourselves at odds with our partner, and separate ourselves from them in our heart. This takes us out of the covenant mode. Suddenly everything is all about me — *my* hurts, *my* rejection, *my* anger over what was done, and *my* right for vindication. In the blink of an eye we have gone from partner (*dead*) to victim (*alive*) and we will divide or separate ourselves from our marriage partner, feeling offended and living in self-preservation. At this point the focus shifts from my partner to me and no one else — a totally selfish, unbiblical, and anti-covenant mode.

> *For where a covenant is, there must of*
> *necessity be the death of the one who*
> *made it. For a covenant is valid*
> *only when men are dead...*
> *Hebrews 9:16-17 NASU*

In Ephesians 5, verses 22-32, Paul writes about marriage, comparing the husband and wife relationship (*covenant*) to the relationship Jesus has with the church. Much like we (*the church*) are in covenant when we are submitted to Him, so the wife is in proper covenant position when she is submitted to her husband. When in this place, she (*the church*) is abiding in Him also (1 Thessalonians 3:24).

> *Wives, be subject to your own husbands,*
> *as to the Lord. For the husband is the*
> *head of the wife, as Christ also is the*
> *head of the church, He Himself being the*
> *Savior of the body. But as the church is*

subject to Christ, so also the wives ought
to be to their husbands in everything.

Ephesians 5:22-24 NASU

In fact, there is a covenant promise made to women who would maintain their covenant position in relation to their husband. This promise is that the Lord would meet the covenant need of *"fixing"* the husband where he may be out of line or disobedient.

In the same way, you wives, be
submissive to your own husbands so that
even if any of them are disobedient to the
word, they may be won without
a word by the behavior of their wives,
as they observe your chaste and
respectful behavior.

1 Peter 3:1-2 NASU

Ephesians 5 continues further to demonstrate the covenantal requirement for the husband to die to himself so he can properly serve his spouse. Much like Jesus laid down His life for us (1 John 3:16), the husband is to lay down his life for his wife. This is because they are one and therefore he would love the wife, even as he loved himself (Matthew 22:39). Now married, he loves her no less than himself and should even prefer her (Philippians 2:3-4) above himself. She is one body with him, and both are members of Christ's body (*one with Him*).

Husbands, love your wives, just as Christ
also loved the church and gave Himself
up for her, so that He might sanctify her,
having cleansed her by the washing of

93

*water with the word, that He might
present to Himself the church in all her
glory, having no spot or wrinkle or any
such thing; but that she would be holy
and blameless. So husbands ought also to
love their own wives as their own bodies.
He who loves his own wife loves himself;
for no one ever hated his own flesh,
but nourishes and cherishes it, just as
Christ also does the church,
because we are members of His body.*

Ephesians 5:25-30 NASU

This is further amplified in First Peter where the Apostle
Peter specifically says that the husband is to treat the wife
as an ***equal covenant partner***. The wording says she is to
be received as a partner or ***fellow heir***. Should he not do
this, he would not be a faithful covenant partner — not just
in respect to his wife, but also to God (Matthew 25:40). As a
result, his needs (*prayers*) would not be met (*answered*).

*You husbands in the same way, live with
your wives in an understanding way,
as with someone weaker, since she is a
woman; and show her honor as a fellow
heir of the grace of life, so that your
prayers will not be hindered.*

1 Peter 3:7 NASU

There are other scriptures that further discuss the depth of the marriage oneness (*such as 1 Corinthians 7*). It says that our bodies are not our own in respect to our spouses, just as our bodies are not our own in respect to the covenant we have with God (*1 Corinthians 6:19-20*).

Now concerning the things about which you wrote, it is good for a man not to touch a woman. But because of immoralities, each man is to have his own wife, and each woman is to have her own husband. The husband must fulfill his duty to his wife, and likewise also the wife to her husband. The wife does not have authority over her own body, but the husband does; and likewise also the husband does not have authority over his own body, but the wife does. Stop depriving one another, except by agreement for a time, so that you may devote yourselves to prayer, and come together again so that Satan will not tempt you because of your lack of self-control.

1 Corinthians 7:1-5 NASU

To withhold anything in the covenant of marriage — whether it be money, sex, or whatever, is definitely a violation of the marriage vows and of the basic principles of covenant. This is what the devil tries to work through unforgiveness between marriage partners, so they will pout, separate, and then justify themselves in withholding.

In fact, one of the real tests in the marriage relationship is whether there can be a relationship free from ought (*offense*). Our partners are not perfect and most likely will not ever be while on earth — and **neither will we**. We must receive them despite their faults and can expect the same from them. In addition, we must not let daily perceptions, careless words, or minor frustrations distract us from our righteous stand as faithful covenant partners. We must not fight flesh and blood, but constantly release our spouses from anything they may have done. We must be quick to repent for any inappropriate behavior on our part. This is the real life "**walk of death**" that keeps us dead to ourselves, keeps the devil out of the middle of our marriage, and keeps the marriage alive on a daily basis.

Just as we see in Psalms 133, there is a blessing that comes from walking in unity in marriage. There is life — covenant life and all it's benefits so the two can stay in that genuine covenant unity.

Behold, how good and how pleasant it is
for brethren to dwell together in unity!

Psalm 133:1 NKJV

Chapter Eight

TAKING THE NAME IN VAIN

You shall not take the name of the LORD
your God in vain, for the LORD
will not leave him unpunished
who takes His name in vain.

Deuteronomy 5:11 NASU

"You shall not take the name of the Lord your God in vain…" What does **that** mean? The third commandment has always bothered me in that I felt I never understood what it actually meant. And, the explanation from most people, never sat comfortably with me.

The general understanding of this commandment seems to be that it has something to do with our using or abusing the Lord's name in our speech. More specifically, it had to do with using the Lord's Name in a cursing or cussing manner. While this certainly is a wrongful use and is sinful, I don't think that this is totally all that the commandment is addressing.

I believe this commandment has been misinterpreted because of ignorance concerning covenant. Unless you read this commandment with a covenant perspective, the meaning will elude you.

In fact, the word '*take*' in verse eleven literally means to lift, to bear, or to carry. The word '*vain*' in the same verse means false, lying, emptiness of speech, or worthlessness. If I put the meanings of these two words together in the context of this verse, I interpret the verse to mean that we are not to bear or carry the Name of the Lord in a false or hypocritical manner. To do so violates the commandment, incurs God's displeasure, and receives an appropriate reaping as a consequence.

I believe this commandment has to do with our covenant vows and our entrance into covenant with Him. In the last chapter, we covered the fact that the bride goes *into* the name of the husband, just as

This commandment should be viewed in context with our covenant vows

we (*the bride*) go *into* the Name of Jesus (*the Bridegroom*) when we are born again and baptized (Matthew 28:19). At this point we take on the Name of the Lord, much like the first step in the ancient ritual of making covenant. We exchange coats with Him. We take Him on — His identity and all that He is (Isaiah 61:10). He takes our old identity from the kingdom of darkness — our sin nature (2 Corinthians 5:21).

Therefore, we become ambassadors of Him (2 Corinthians 5:20) with a ministry of reconciliation and a purpose to include good works He ordained beforehand (Ephesians 2:10). We should look like Him because our very nature has changed and we become more like Him. This includes our covenant obligation to abide in Him, which is fulfilled through our obedience (1 John 3:24; John 15:14).

Our unrighteousness (*or disobedience*) would therefore reflect poorly on Him and the kingdom of God, and not be in consonance with His will for us (1 Thessalonians 4:3).

This would be a bad witness of Him and His purpose for us, and the kingdom as well (Matthew 6:10).

Isaiah 4:1 speaks to this situation where people want all the covenant benefits without any covenant obligations. In other words, they want covenant on their terms, not God's. They don't want to die or change their identities (*exchange coats*) or eat of the bread of life, but they want all the benefits from covenant living.

> *For seven women will take hold of one man in that day, saying, "We will eat our own bread and wear our own clothes, only let us be called by your name; take away our reproach!"*
>
> *Isaiah 4:1 NASU*

We see a similar situation with the church at Laodicea. Found in the the Book of Revelation, chapter three, the Laodiceans are going around seemingly prosperous and therefore happy in the natural. They probably attend church and fulfill all the religious requirements, but are deceived about the truth. They think they are okay with God because they are "blessed" financially. Little do they know they are not properly clothed spiritually and are severely wanting — in spite of all the outward prosperity.

> *To the angel of the church in Laodicea write:*
>
> *The Amen, the faithful and true Witness, the Beginning of the creation of God, says this:*

"I know your deeds,
that you are neither cold nor hot;
I wish that you were cold or hot.

"So because you are lukewarm,
and neither hot nor cold,
I will spit you out of My mouth.

"Because you say, 'I am rich, and have
become wealthy, and have need of
nothing,' and you do not know that you
are wretched and miserable and poor
and blind and naked, I advise you to buy
from Me gold refined by fire so that you
may become rich, and white garments so
that you may clothe yourself, and that
the shame of your nakedness will not be
revealed; and eye salve to anoint your
eyes so that you may see.

Rev 3:14-19 NASU

The truth in this passage also explains another scripture
that many have difficulty with.

Not everyone who says to Me, "Lord,
Lord," will enter the kingdom of heaven,
but he who does the will of My Father
who is in heaven will enter.

Many will say to Me on that day,
"Lord, Lord, did we not prophesy in Your
name, and in Your name

*cast out demons, and in Your name
perform many miracles?"*

*And then I will declare to them,
"I never knew you;
DEPART FROM ME,
YOU WHO PRACTICE LAWLESSNESS."
Matthew 7:21-23 NASU*

Notice that the whole issue surrounds doing the will of the Father. This involves being obedient and walking in covenant with the Lord. Being in a situation like the one in Isaiah 4:1 or Revelations 3: 14-18 puts someone in a position of not abiding, of not being totally in fellowship, and not totally committed to Him and His ways. Therefore, all that they supposedly do for the Lord or for the kingdom of God is in vain. In fact, they are **bearing** or **carrying** the name in vain.

If we are born again, then we will change and are continually in the process of being changed. We should be looking more and more like the Lord and His Word with each passing day. As we grow, our character should be improved and we should be displaying the fruits of the Spirit — because the Holy Spirit lives in us and is guiding (*changing*) us (Romans 8:11-14). That is why the fruits of the flesh are a clear indication that someone is not born again, and the fruits of the Spirit are indicative of someone who is (Galatians 5).

Claiming to be born again, but looking and acting like the world is inconsistent. This behavior would reflect one who wants the benefits of covenant, but doesn't want to walk a covenant walk. This is a person who would take the Name in vain — one who was not a good witness, one who was not a true ambassador, one who reflected poorly on both Jesus and His kingdom. In accordance with Deuteronomy 5:11, this is a person who will be punished as a result.

> *...for the LORD*
> *will not leave him unpunished*
> *who takes His name in vain.*
>
> *Deuteronomy 5:11 NASU*

The word *'punished'* in the verse above (*NASU*) is translated as *'guiltless'* in the King James Version and means; innocent, cleansed, purged, acquitted. So we see that the one who takes the Name in vain **is not** innocent, but is guilty and will be appropriately judged (*reap consequences*). With this clearly in our minds, we must be careful to **follow** and **do** what the Lord directs us to do (John 10:27). Obedience is an indicator of true sheep — true followers, and those who reflect properly on the Lord and His kingdom.

Chapter Nine

COVENANT TERMS/WORDS

There are a number of words/terms in both the Old and New Testament that have covenant implications. When you see them you will greatly appreciate this understanding, as the covenant aspect will certainly enrich your study of the scriptures involved. The ones listed here repesent a small sample and are by no means meant to be conclusive.

FRIEND

This is not just an acquaintance as the term '*friend*' has come to mean today in our culture. In ancient cultures, a friend was a covenant partner who was closer than the blood relative (Proverbs 18:24). This term also includes a spouse who becomes a blood covenant 'brother' through marriage. In John 15:14, there is a strong statement about our covenant relationship with the Lord that defines our part in keeping covenant — *"You are my friend if you do what I command you."*

FRIEND*S*HIP

This means a covenant relationship, not a casual relationship. In fact, in the book of James we see this term as an implied reference to the exchange of belts and weapons from the covenant ritual — meaning my friends are your friends, and my enemies are your enemies, and vice versa. James 4:4 says, *"Friendship with the world is enmity to God."*

RIGHT HAND

This reference comes directly from the covenant ritual whereby the two making covenant bind their right hands, wrists and arms together, allowing the blood from the incisions to flow into each other's bodies. The right hand is a symbol of strength as the covenant partner is your *'backup'* strength should he be needed. It is interesting to note that the handshake originated from this covenant ritual and was often used to seal business deals — even in modern times. Jesus, Who made covenant for us, sat down at the **right hand** of the Father.

GRACE

This term is strongly covenantal in that His grace is there to cover us and is freely given to meet our every need. It states in 2 Corinthians 12:9-10 that His grace is sufficient, and that where we are weak, He is strong. The Bible also says in James 4:6 that He gives grace to the humble — that is, to those who come under His Lordship, assuming their proper covenant position as a *'friend.'* As we give way to Him, submit and are obedient to what He is saying and doing, He will give us grace — empower us to do it.

ABIDE

This is a reference to walking in right covenant standing with the Lord. In John 15 it refers to us abiding in Him and He abiding in us. This is a reference to the oneness of covenant. In addition, 1 John 3:24, states what our part of keeping covenant is — that we abide in Him by keeping His commandments.

IN HIS NAME — IN THE NAME OF JESUS

These phrases strongly relate to covenant. When we are in covenant we are *in His Name*. We get baptized *into the Name* in water baptism (Matthew 28:19; Romans 6:3). If a number of us are gathered together and are in good covenant standing (*obedient to Him/in His Name*), then He has promised that He will be in our midst (Matthew 18: 19-20) and what we pray will come to pass (John 16:23-24).

ONENESS/UNITY

This specifically suggests covenant unity, since when two go into covenant, they are no longer two, but are now one — as in marriage. This is also illustrated in John 17:20-24, where we see the Father and Son as one, and Christians (*the Lord's covenant people*) as one with them. It is this oneness that precipitates life (*His presence*) and brings the blessings that come with Him (Psalms 133).

NEEDS

This oftentimes has to do with covenant, in that covenant people are required to meet each other's needs (*though not necessarily their wants*). This can be seen in 1 John 3:16-18 where it says that our basic covenant love should drive us to meet any such need. Paul also lauds those who met his needs in Philippians 4:19, asking a covenant God to meet their needs in exchange.

LORD'S SUPPER

This is a covenant memorial meal that is reminiscent of the original ancient covenant ritual. Today God's covenant people take the Lord's Supper as a remembrance of what He did for us at the cross when He made covenant for us. 1 Corithians 11:27-30 tells us that we need to be in good covenant standing with Him and our fellow Christians when taking the covenant meal or some may get sick — even sleep (*die*).

BLESSINGS AND CURSES

These are a result of keeping or breaking covenant. So, in actuality we determine through our choices whether we receive life or death, blessings or curses in our lives and in the lives of our descendants (Deuteronomy 30:19-20). Our obedience is a requirement for us to be in good covenant standing. That's why it says in Deuteronomy 28:2 that blessings will overtake us if we diligently obey.

OBEDIENCE

This is a covenant requirement. We vow, going into covenant, that He is Lord. This makes us subservient to His will and wishes. We are in good covenant standing when we maintain Him as Lord in our life through our obedience. That's why it says that we abide in Him when we keep His commandments (1 John 3:24).

THE BATTLE IS THE LORD'S

This means that He will fight our battles if we are in good covenant standing. He is our covenant Friend and will be strong and fight our enemies — our enemies become His enemies due to covenant. That is also why it says in Zechariah 4:6, *"not by might nor by power, but by My Spirit, says the Lord of hosts."*

LIFTING HANDS

When covenant was made in ancient days, the covenant scars on the wrists were purposely roughed up and made easy to see. So, when an enemy approached, the covenant partner would raise his hands to display the covenant scars. This was a sign or a warning to the one approaching that this person lifting their hands was protected by a covenant friend. When we praise and lift our hands, we remind ourselves and show others that we are in covenant with the Lord. In fact, Jesus' wrists were scarred, or pierced through for us. In 1 Timothy 2:8, we see the hands are to be lifted without wrath or dissention. This means that we are to be in good covenant relationship with our brothers and sisters.

DYING TO SELF

This is a covenant requirement for all covenant partners. Jesus laid down His life for us, and we should lay down our life for the brethren (1 John 3:16). This covenant walk is a walk of death — dying to ourselves and living for the kingdom which would be for Him and our other covenant brothers. In fact, it says in Hebrews 9:16 that a covenant is valid only when men are dead.

LOAF/ BREAD

There is covenant meaning and symbolism in the loaf of bread. The implication from 1 Corinthians 10:16-17 is that we are (*as a body*) one loaf, and we each are a piece of that loaf — each being a part of the body of Christ. In 1 Corinthians 5 we are warned that a little leaven, leavens the whole loaf. This reference speaks to the destruction that sin can do in a corporate covenant body, so the sin (*or leaven*) has to be removed.

PUT ON THE ARMOR OF GOD

Notice that it is **His** armor and not ours. In other words, we are to be strong in Him and the power of His might (Ephesians 6:10). Just like the exchange of weapons and belts in the covenant ritual (1 Samuel 18:1-4), we have His strength behind us and His ability to fight in defending ourselves. The weapons of our warfare are not carnal, but divinely powerful (2 Corinthians 10:4).

HE IS MY TOWER, MY STRENGTH, MY REFUGE

These terms appear a number of places, particularly in Psalms. They are totally covenant in that Jesus becomes these things to us whenever we abide in Him (*in covenant*). We are no longer vulnerable, weak, or insecure when we have exchanged our weakness for His strengths and abilities.

BRUCE GUNKLE

Apostle Bruce Gunkle is a graduate of the U.S. Naval Academy who attained the rank of full colonel while on active duty. He retired with 21 years of honorable service. Bruce now pastors the City of Refuge Christian Fellowship in San Antonio, Texas. His wife of 41 years, Sherry, is a prophetess and functions as the worship leader for the City of Refuge as well as for national conferences. Together they have two daughters and three grandchildren.

The City of Refuge is a prophetic, apostolic church that encourages all its members to be actively involved in the harvest and kingdom work. Bruce believes strongly in the local church and is an ardent proponent of training up and releasing people to do the work of Jesus — building kingdom people who will change their families, impact their city and change the world! Bruce's insight and revelation are refreshing; challenging traditions and confronting the false sense of comfort created by belief in a watered down presentation of God's Word. Bruce is committed to the truth of God's Word and makes no attempt to dilute or sugar coat the truth.

The City of Refuge seeks to be attentive to what the Spirit is saying to the church in these last days. There is a strong prophetic flow and presence that characterizes every worship service. It is also a place of healing where inner healing and deliverance are emphasized. Many, including five fold ministers and their spouses, have found refuge there, having been released from the bondages that have hindered them in fulfilling their kingdom work.

Bruce relates apostolically to a number of pastors and churches in this country and one in Mexico City. His wisdom is sought by many ministers who have learned to trust the strong discernment and understanding that distinguish his ministry.

With a strong commitment to influencing his region with the kingdom of God, Bruce remains active in many local city events.

APOSTLE BRUCE GUNKLE

**City of Refuge Christian Fellowship
1201 Austin Hwy Ste 116
San Antonio, TX 78209**

(210) 829-1792

*www.thecityofrefuge.org
bgunkle@hotmail.com*

TEST FOR COVENANT KEEPING

The purpose of this exercise is to see if you generally understand covenant, and whether you are abiding in it, as best you know how.

1. Do you meet the genuine needs of your brothers and sisters in Christ when you recognize these needs? *I John 3:16-18; Acts 2:44-45; Acts 4:34*

2. Are you obedient to the Lord and His Word? *John 15:14; John 14:15; John 10:27*

3. Do you tend to please (serve) men rather than God? *Galatians 1:10; Luke 12:4-6; Matthew 4:10*

4. Would you correct/admonish a brother who is in error/sin, regardless of whether it would jeopardize your friendship? *Proverbs 27:6; James 5:19-20*

5. Are you in submission to those in authority over you as best you know? *Romans 13: 1-2; James 4:7*

6. Are you easily offended? *I Corinthians 13:4-7; I John 20-21; Matthew 25:40*

7. Are you prejudiced or partial in any of your dealings with people? *Galatians 3:28; Matthew 22:39*

8. Do you discipline your children in accordance with scriptural guidelines? *Proverbs 22:6; Galatians 1:10; Matthew 10:37*

9. Does fear prevent you from stepping out when you should? *II Timothy 1:7; Nehemiah 6:13; Matthew 25:25-26*

10. Do you easily get frustrated or angry with others? *James 1:20; I Corinthians 13:4-7; Ephesians 6:12*

11. Do you normally have to have your own way?
    Philippians 2:3-4; Matthew 22:39; I John 3:16

12. Is the impact of money often the overriding factor in your daily decisions? *I Timothy 6:10; Matthew 6:24; Matthew 19:21-27*

13. Do you have a problem forgiving others?
    Matthew 6:14-15; I Corinthians 13:4-7

14. Do you tend to be worldly/carnal rather than practice righteousness? *Isaiah 61:10; James 4:4; I John 3:6-8*

15. As an adult, do the preferences of your parents/family override what you know God wants you to do?
    Matthew 10:37; Luke 12:4-6; Matthew 19:29

16. Have you spoken against a brother in Christ?
    Matthew 25:40; James 4:11

17. Do you honor your wife as a fellow heir?
    I Peter 3:7

18. Do you withhold your body from your spouse?
    I Corinthians 7: 3-5

19. Have you been faithful in repaying loans/debts, or any other written or verbal contracts?
    Deuteronomy 5:11; Matthew 25:40; James 5:4

20. Are you committed to and tithe to a local church?
    Hebrews 10:24-25; Proverbs 18:1; John 17:21-23